P O C K E T S

HORSES

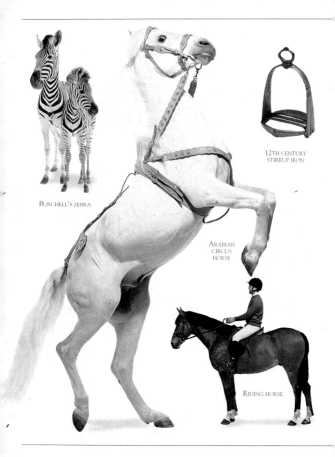

BURCHELL'S ZEBRA

12TH CENTURY
STIRRUP IRON

ARABIAN
CIRCUS
HORSE

RIDING HORSE

P O C K E T S
HORSES

Written by
DAVID ALDERTON

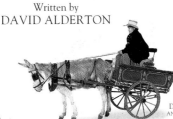

DONKEY
AND TRAP

SHIRE
HORSE

MOUNTED
POLICE OFFICER

SHETLAND
PONY

DK PUBLISHING

LONDON, NEW YORK,
MELBOURNE, MUNICH, and DELHI

Project editor Alan Burrows
Art editor Carole Oliver
Senior editor Laura Buller
Senior art editor Helen Senior
Picture research Anna Lord
Production Louise Barratt
US editor Jill Hamilton
US consultant Sharon Ralls Lemon

REVISED EDITION
Project editor Steve Setford
Designer Sarah Crouch
Managing editor Linda Esposito
Managing art editor Jane Thomas
DTP designer Siu Yin Ho
Consultant David Alderton
Production Erica Rosen
US editors Margaret Parrish, Christine Heilman

Second American Edition, 2003
Published in the United States by
DK Publishing, Inc., 375 Hudson Street,
New York, New York 10014

08 10 9 8 7

A Cataloging-in-Publication record for the First American Edition of this book
is available from the Library of Congress.

ISBN-13: 978-0-7894-9588-4

Color reproduction by Colourscan, Singapore
Printed and bound in Italy by L.E.G.O.

See our complete product line at
www.dk.com

CONTENTS

HOW TO USE THIS BOOK

These pages show you how to use *Pockets: Horses*.
The book is divided into several sections. The main
sections consist of information on different breeds of
horse. There is also an introductory section at the
front, and a reference section at the back. Each new
section begins with a picture page, which gives an
idea of what it is about.

HORSE TYPES

The horses in the book are arranged
into four main types: ponies, light
horses, heavy horses, and wild and
feral horses. Each type features
recognized breeds. Often, other
breeds, which are considered as
influences, are also included.

Corner coding

Heading

Introduction

LIGHT HORSES

CLEVELAND BAY

DESCENDED FROM the English Yorkshire Coach
Horses of the 1800s, these versatile workers pull
royal carriages on state occasions. The horses are
called Cleveland Bays
because they originally
came from Cleveland on
the northeastern coast of
England. They are
characterized by a
distinctive bay-
colored coat with a
black mane and tail.

Muscular neck and sloping shoulders provide power

ROYAL CARRIAGE HORSES
The Cleveland Bays used in England to pull the
royal carriages are kept in the Royal Mews near
Buckingham Palace in London. At one time, the
Duke of Edinburgh raced a team of part Cleveland
Bays in driving competitions.

94

No feathering on the heels

Size indicator

CORNER CODING

Corners of horse and
pony pages are color
coded with yellow, blue,
red, and green to
remind you which
section you are in.

☐ PONIES

☐ LIGHT HORSES

☐ HEAVY HORSES

☐ WILD AND
FERAL HORSES

HEADING

This describes the
subject of the page.
This page is about the
Cleveland Bay. If a
subject continues over
several pages, the
same heading applies.

INTRODUCTION

This provides a clear,
general overview of the
subject, and gives key
information that you need
to know about it.

CAPTIONS AND
ANNOTATIONS

Each illustration has a
caption. Annotations, in
italics, point out features of
an illustration.

8

RUNNING HEADS
These remind you which section you are in. The top of the left-hand page gives the section name. The right-hand page gives the subject. This page comes from the section on light horses.

FACT BOXES
Many pages have fact boxes. These contain at-a-glance information about the horse featured on that page. This fact box gives interesting facts about the history of the Cleveland Bay.

SIZE INDICATORS
These show the average height of the horse is measured in hands. One hand is equal to 4 in (10 cm), the approximate breadth of a large hand.

16

Caption   Running head

RECORDS AND FACTS

CLEVELAND BAY

BAVARIAN WARMBLOOD
In the late 1700s, Cleveland Bays helped the development of the Bavarian Warmblood, giving it strength and stamina. This German breed is kept as a competition and carriage horse.

Tail is usually black, but grey hairs are a sign of purity.

CLEVELAND BAY FACTS
• Cleveland Bays used to be called Chapman Horses after traveling salesmen (chapmen) who used these horses to pull their carts.
• In 1962, Queen Elizabeth II bought and bred one of the last four stallions to save the breed from extinction.
• Cleveland Bays have been used as plow and draft horses on farms, as packhorses, and for carrying coal.

Powerful quarters help the horse jump well

Long legs give the horse plenty of height

Annotation   Fact box

REFERENCE SECTION
The reference section pages are yellow and appear at the back of the book. On these, you will find useful facts, figures, and charts. These pages give horse records, such as the biggest and smallest, and important horse care information.

LABELS
For greater clarity, some pictures have labels. They may give extra information, or identify a picture when it is not obvious from the text what it is.

INDEX
You will find an index at the back of Pockets: Horses. This acts as a species and a subject index. Every subject and type of horse covered in the book is listed alphabetically.

9

INTRODUCTION
TO HORSES

WHAT IS A HORSE?

SOME 60 MILLION YEARS AGO the first horses ran on the plains of North America. The modern horse has single-hooved feet and a greater length of leg than its earlier ancestors. Like all mammals, horses suckle their young, and as herbivores, their natural food is grass. They are social creatures, and prefer to live in groups.

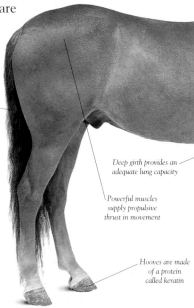

Long tail helps to keep flies off the body

Deep girth provides an adequate lung capacity

Powerful muscles supply propulsive thrust in movement

Hooves are made of a protein called keratin

HORSE FACTS

• Horses are measured from the ground up to the withers, which is the highest point of the shoulders.

• In 1910, North America had about 20 million domestic horses.

• There are over 150 officially recognized horse and pony breeds.

• Most modern horse breeds have been deliberately created to do a specific task.

1 2

Long hair on the back of the neck is called a mane

Horses have an excellent sense of hearing

Withers

Long head and neck allow horse to graze while standing

It takes over two years for a horse foal to take on adult proportions

Long legs developed to run from danger

HORSES AND HUMANS
As this cave painting shows, early humans hunted horses for their meat and skin. By keeping horses in herds, these essential items became more readily available. Eventually, horses were used for riding and pulling carts, and later they were bred to perform all kinds of work.

BORN TO RUN
Both wild and domestic horses give birth to fully developed offspring. This is because in the wild the young foal must keep up with its mother and the herd, as well as escaping from predators.

THE HORSE IN HISTORY

DOMESTICATION OF HORSES began in Asia about 5,000 to 6,000 years ago. Originally this provided tribes with meat, milk, hides, and helped to increase their mobility. Horses were later used to pull loads and then chariots. This led to horsepower becoming a vital component in transportation and warfare.

Horse

Hinny

BEFORE HORSES
Oxen or onagers were domesticated before horses. This Mesopotamian mosaic of 2500 BC shows a team of onagers pulling a chariot.

CHARIOTS
After horse-riding tribes made contact with the Egyptians, horses and hinnies (the offspring of a male horse and a female donkey) became a popular means of transportation in Egypt. Both animals are painted on this Egyptian tomb of c.1400 BC.

MYTHOLOGICAL STORIES
According to ancient Greek
mythology, Pegasus, a winged
horse, rose from the severed head
of the gorgon Medusa. Athena, goddess
of wisdom, caught it and tamed it with
a golden bridle. Later, Greek
astronomers gave the name
Pegasus to a group of stars
in the northern sky.

CONSTELLATION
OF PEGASUS

HUNTING FOR PLEASURE
Horses have been used for
hunting for centuries. This mosaic is from
late 5th or 6th century North Africa.

6TH CENTURY
PERSIAN PLATE

EMPIRE BUILDERS
In the 6th century,
Persians used horses to
create the first sizable
empire. The Persians
were excellent riders
and defeated their
enemies with horse-
drawn chariots and
cavalry. They also built
roads and set up an
efficient postal system,
relying on horses, to help
them run their domain.

More horses in history

Before the arrival of the steam engine, just about everything was moved by horses. People traveled in carts and carriages, and goods went by pack horses on roads or by horse-drawn barges on canals. In war, horses were used in cavalry formations and for the movement of guns and supplies. Horses were popular as children's toys, much in the same way as cars are today.

BARGE HORSES
The first canal barges in the 18 century were pulled by horses on a towpath beside the water Loads of up to 50 tons (45 tonne were hauled at speeds of about 2 mph (3.3 km/h).

JOUSTING
In 15th-century Europe, mounted knights prepared for war by jousting. In this sport, a knight tried to unhorse his opponent or break his own lance against the other's shield. A fully loaded jousting horse carried around 419 lb (190 kg) of knight, armor, and saddle.

Brightly colored caparison covers horse

Leather gauntlet o glove

Heavy chain mail armor

HISTORICAL FACTS
• El Cid, the Christian warrior, called his horse *Babieca*, the Spanish word for "stupid."
• A "freelance" was a medieval mercenary with a horse and lance.
• An Austrian horse-drawn railroad opened in 1852; it was 124 miles (200 km) long.

19TH CENTURY
PHAETON CARRIAGE

*Phaetons were
pulled by either one
or two horses*

CITY TRANSPORTATION

Before the early 20th century,
much of the transportation
in cities was horse-
powered. Horses pulled
cabs, buses, trams, and
private carriages. The
phaeton was a light,
four-wheeled vehicle
that was designed to be
driven by its owner. It
became fashionable in the
19th century.

*Metal helm, the largest and
heaviest type of helmet*

18TH-CENTURY
ROCKING
HORSE

TOYS

As the horse played such a
large part in everyday life, it
naturally became popular as a
children's toy. Rocking
horses were
invented in the
early 1600s.

*Wooden lance
up to 8 ft
(2.5 m) long has
blunted tip to
prevent injury*

*Saddle has a high
back to help absorb
shock of impact*

THE FIRST HORSES

THE ORIGINS OF today's horses can be traced back over 60 million years. The first horses probably started to evolve in what is now the southeastern part of North America, before the continents split and moved to their present positions. Horses became extinct there about 8,000 years ago, but thrived in Asia, Africa, and Europe.

HIPPARION
This was the last of the three-toed horses. Its remains have been found in Europe, Asia, and Africa, where it lived up to 15,000 years ago.

SKULL
Small teeth ideal for browsing

FOUR-TOED FOOT
Four toes on front feet good for marshy land

EOHIPPUS
This small browsing animal, no bigger than a hare, was the ancestor of the modern horse. It became extinct about 40 million years ago.

SKULL
Narrow jaw and longer head

THREE-TOED FOOT
Fewer toes better for running on hard ground

MESOHIPPUS
As the forests began to thin out, and the land became drier and harder, early horses such as *Mesohippus* could run and trot over long distances.

SKULL
Incisor teeth begin to develop

THREE-TOED FOOT
Outside toes are still prominent

MIOHIPPUS
This was a more advanced form of *Mesohippus* and lived around 30 million years ago. It had still to develop the galloping action of modern horses.

ORIGINS

Land bridges helped horses to establish their present distribution. The Bering land bridge between North America and Asia was cut at the end of the last Ice Age because of the rising sea level. This separated the populations of horses.

Bering land bridge

60 MILLION YEARS AGO

PRESENT DAY

FIRST HORSE FACTS

• Scientists suspect that a disease wiped out the early North American horses.

• The first *Eohippus* was discovered in 1867 in Wyoming.

• The wild ancestral horses of South America are all extinct.

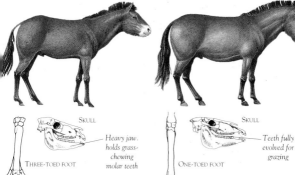

SKULL

SKULL

Heavy jaw holds grass-chewing molar teeth

THREE-TOED FOOT

Teeth fully evolved for grazing

ONE-TOED FOOT

Two side toes are kept off the ground and body is supported by central toe

First single hoof of today's modern breeds

MERYCHIPPUS

A long neck helped *Merychippus* graze, rather than browse. This horse lived on the prairies of present-day Nebraska, in the North American midwest, about 15 million years ago.

PLIOHIPPUS

The direct ancestor of the modern horse, *Pliohippus* lived about six million years ago. It had the general proportions of today's equines and stood around 48 in (122 cm) high at the shoulder.

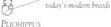

MAIN HORSE TYPES

MOST MODERN HORSES are thought to be descended from four types which inhabited Europe and Asia over 6,000 years ago. Their features can still be seen in some breeds today. Domestication led to the variety of modern breeds and their spread across the world.

Broad forehead with straight profile

Lean with narrow body

PONY TYPE 1
This hardy pony looked similar to today's Exmoor breed of Great Britain. It lived in northwestern Europe.

HORSE TYPE 1
Originating from central Asia, this horse lived in dry, arid conditions and resembled the modern Akhal-Teke.

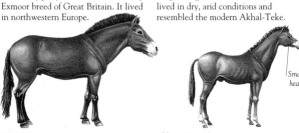

Small head

PONY TYPE 2
Similar to Przewalski's horse, the Type 2 was powerfully built with a heavy head and roamed over northern Eurasia.

HORSE TYPE 2
Living in the hot deserts of western Asia, this slim horse was possibly the ancestor of the Arabian and Caspian.

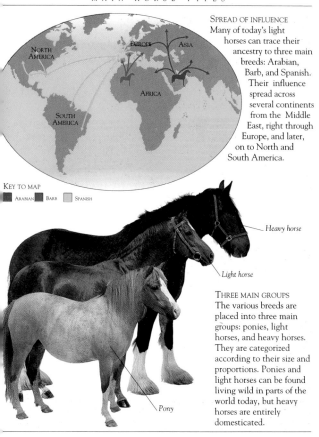

SPREAD OF INFLUENCE
Many of today's light
horses can trace their
ancestry to three main
breeds: Arabian,
Barb, and Spanish.
Their influence
spread across
several continents
from the Middle
East, right through
Europe, and later,
on to North and
South America.

KEY TO MAP

■ ARABIAN ■ BARB □ SPANISH

Heavy horse

Light horse

THREE MAIN GROUPS
The various breeds are
placed into three main
groups: ponies, light
horses, and heavy horses.
They are categorized
according to their size and
proportions. Ponies and
light horses can be found
living wild in parts of the
world today, but heavy
horses are entirely
domesticated.

Pony

BODY AND CONFORMATION

A HORSE'S BODY IS perfectly designed for its way of life. The neck is long so it can stoop to graze, and long, muscular legs allow it to run away from danger. The proportions of a horse's body, or conformation, may vary according to the group or breed.

Points

The external features of a horse are called the points. Each point has a different name and together they make up the horse's conformation.

Mane

Crest

Withers

Throat

Jugular groove

Poll

Neck

Ear

Eye

Forehead

Shoulder

Breast

Facial crest

Nasal bone

Knee joint

Cannon bone

Cheek

Nostril

Lower jaw

Muzzle

Fetlock joint

Upper lip

Lower lip

PROPORTION
In a perfectly proportioned horse, certain measurements of the body should all be equal. Those shown in blue should correspond to each other, as should the lines drawn in both red and gray.

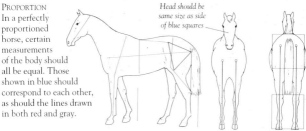

Head should be same size as side of blue squares

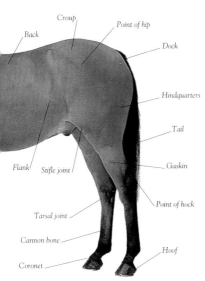

Croup

Back

Point of hip

Dock

Hindquarters

Tail

Gaskin

Flank   Stifle joint

Point of hock

Tarsal joint

Cannon bone

Coronet

Hoof

FRONT AND REAR LIMBS
When viewed from the front, a line from the shoulder should pass through the center of the knees, fetlock, and foot. A straight line should also pass through the rear legs.

ANATOMICAL FACTS

• The body and head of a horse are streamlined and this helps to reduce wind resistance.

• A long neck and well-sloped shoulders may indicate that the horse is fast and good for riding.

• Large eyes usually show not only that the horse has good vision, but also a calm nature and intelligence.

Skeleton and muscles

The framework of the horse consists of a skeleton, made up of a number of connected bones that are moved by muscles. Along the spinal, or vertebral, column, which runs from the head to the tail, is the spinal cord – the connection between the horse's brain and body. When a horse wants to move, it sends a message from its brain down the cord via nerves to signal the appropriate muscle.

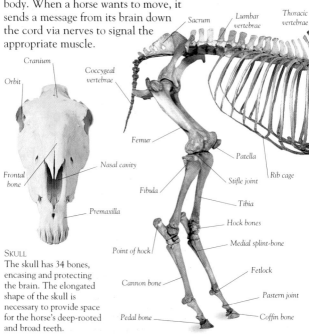

Cranium

Orbit

Frontal bone

Nasal cavity

Premaxilla

Coccygeal vertebrae

Sacrum

Lumbar vertebrae

Thoracic vertebrae

Femur

Patella

Stifle joint

Rib cage

Fibula

Tibia

Hock bones

Point of hock

Medial splint-bone

Cannon bone

Fetlock

Pastern joint

Pedal bone

Coffin bone

SKULL
The skull has 34 bones, encasing and protecting the brain. The elongated shape of the skull is necessary to provide space for the horse's deep-rooted and broad teeth.

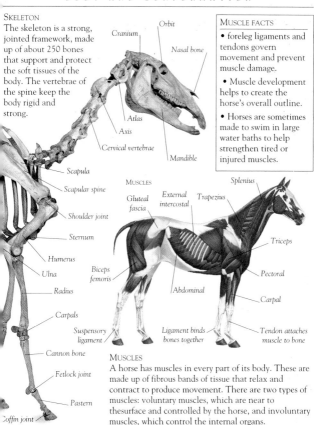

SKELETON
The skeleton is a strong, jointed framework, made up of about 250 bones that support and protect the soft tissues of the body. The vertebrae of the spine keep the body rigid and strong.

Orbit

Cranium

Nasal bone

Atlas

Axis

Cervical vertebrae

Mandible

Scapula

Scapular spine

Shoulder joint

Sternum

Humerus

Ulna

Radius

Carpals

Suspensory ligament

Cannon bone

Fetlock joint

Pastern

Coffin joint

MUSCLE FACTS
• foreleg ligaments and tendons govern movement and prevent muscle damage.
• Muscle development helps to create the horse's overall outline.
• Horses are sometimes made to swim in large water baths to help strengthen tired or injured muscles.

MUSCLES

Splenius

Gluteal fascia

External intercostal

Trapezius

Triceps

Biceps femoris

Pectoral

Abdominal

Carpal

Ligament binds bones together

Tendon attaches muscle to bone

MUSCLES
A horse has muscles in every part of its body. These are made up of fibrous bands of tissue that relax and contract to produce movement. There are two types of muscles: voluntary muscles, which are near to thesurface and controlled by the horse, and involuntary muscles, which control the internal organs.

COAT COLORS

HORSES COME IN a variety of colors,
patterns, and markings. Some breeds
include horses of different colors, while
others, such as the Palomino, are
defined as breeds primarily by the
color of their body, mane, and tail,
and certain distinguishing marks.

UNIQUE PATTERN
The zebra's striped
pattern consists of black
stripes on a white coat.

GRAY
White and black hairs,
over black skin.

FLEABITTEN
Gray coat, flecked with
brown specks of hair.

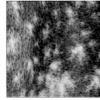

DAPPLE GRAY
Gray base, with rings
made of dark gray hairs.

PALOMINO
Gold, with white mane
and tail; little black.

CHESTNUT
Golden, varying from pale
to rich reddish gold.

LIVER CHESTNUT
Darkest possible shade of
chestnut coloring.

BAY
Reddish brown to dark
gold, with black points.

BROWN
Black and brown, with
black mane, tail, and legs.

BLACK
Solid black, sometimes
with small white marks.

STRAWBERRY-ROAN
Chestnut body color,
mixed with white hairs.

BLUE ROAN
Black or brown coat hairs
mixed with some white.

DUN
Either yellow, blue, or
mousebrown color.

SPOTTED
Small spots; sometimes
termed Appaloosa color.

SKEWBALD
Base color broken by large
patches of white.

PIEBALD
Black and white patches
in no fixed pattern.

Patterns and markings

Individual horses can be identified by body markings, which can be either natural or acquired. Natural markings are often areas of white hair on the head, legs, and hooves. Acquired markings are the result of branding or injury. Branding has been carried out for more than 2,000 years and can help to identify the horse if it is stolen.

FACE MARKINGS
While some breeds are defined by their coat patterns, face markings help to identify individual horses. The most common face markings are named below.

BLAZE

WHITE MUZZLE

SNIP

LIP MARKS

WHITE FACE

STRIPE

STAR AND STRIPE

STAR

ERMINE   SOCK   STOCKING   ZEBRA

LEG MARKINGS

These markings are often white. They are called ermine if they are just above the hoof, a sock if they extend below the knee, and a stocking when extending above the knee. Zebra markings are dark rings.

HOOF MARKINGS

The blue hoof is made of hard blue horn and is most often associated with ponies. Hooves of black and white vertical stripes are seen on the Appaloosa and other spotted horse breeds.

BLUE HOOF   STRIPED HOOF

DORSAL STRIPE

This mark extends from the tail to the withers. It is found on primitive horses such as the Tarpan, and is associated with dun-colored coats.

IDENTITY MARKINGS

Artificial markings help identify ownership and sometimes breed. Brand marks are applied by a hot iron rod which stops the hair from growing back. Freeze marks are frozen on in a similar way.

BRAND MARK   FREEZE MARK

MOVEMENT

HORSES HAVE FOUR TYPES of movement, called paces. These are the walk, trot, canter, and gallop. The walk is the slowest pace. The horse can then accelerate to a trot, going faster still when cantering. Running at top speed is galloping. In every case, the hooves touch down in a different sequence called a gait.

ACTION
The word describes the movement of the skeletal frame in locomotion. The sequence of footfalls is different for each gait; the walk is a four-beat gait, trot is two, and canter three.

Slope of shoulders directly influences movement

A horse walks at abo 3–5 mph (8 km/h) and can gallop for short distances up t 40 mph (60 km/h)

WALKING
When a horse walks, it places its four legs on the ground in regular succession. The strides are of equal distance and their length depends on the size of the horse and its conformation.

On left-handed turns a horse "leads" at canter and gallop with the left foreleg and vice versa

JUMPING

The horse uses its hindlegs to power its leap forward and upward. As it jumps, it folds its legs under its body, then stretches down, touching the ground with one foreleg, immediately followed by the other.

Legs are folded under body to avoid obstacles

HARDY BREED

The Criollo from Argentina is often regarded as the most robust breed in the world. Descended from Spanish stock, it is tough and capable of great endurance.

Horses will instinctively jump obstructions

A foal can keep up with its mother within hours of its birth

MOVEMENT FACTS

• Ponies lift their feet and have a higher knee action, being adapted to life on much rougher terrain.

• Light horses hardly bend their knees. This allows each stride to cover more ground.

• A straighter angle in the shoulder of a heavy horse gives shorter, elevated strides with more pulling power.

FOOD AND DIET

LIKE ANY ANIMAL, horses get their energy from food. They are herbivores, which means they do not eat meat. In the wild, horses can survive on grass and herbs as long as their grazing area is large enough. In the winter, when it is cold and there is less food, wild horses get out of condition, while in the summer they put on weight.

FIRST SOLID FOOD
Young horses are able to eat their first solid food from about six weeks.

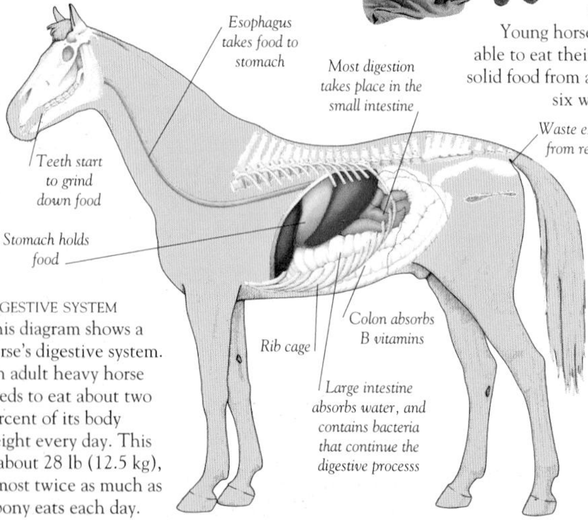

Esophagus takes food to stomach

Most digestion takes place in the small intestine

Waste expelled from rectum

Teeth start to grind down food

Stomach holds food

Colon absorbs B vitamins

Rib cage

Large intestine absorbs water, and contains bacteria that continue the digestive processs

DIGESTIVE SYSTEM
This diagram shows a horse's digestive system. An adult heavy horse needs to eat about two percent of its body weight every day. This is about 28 lb (12.5 kg), almost twice as much as a pony eats each day.

TEETH AND JAWS

Grazing wears down the foal's milk teeth and by the time the horse is five, these are replaced by a set of 40 adult teeth. The incisors cut the food into small pieces and the molars grind it down, ready for digestion.

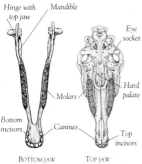

Hinge with top jaw

Mandible

Eye socket

Molars

Hard palate

Bottom incisors

Canines

Top incisors

BOTTOM JAW

TOP JAW

BALANCED DIET

Horses need a balanced diet, with enough vitamins and minerals to help them stay healthy and in condition. Horses should be fed little and often. Water with the meal keeps the horse from becoming dehydrated.

Fruit and root vegetables must be chopped up lengthwise so the horse does not choke.

Feed bowl holds carrots, corn, linseed, nuts, chaff, and a slice of apple

Hay is grass that has been cut and dried.

Bucket of clean, fresh water

FOOD DANGERS

• Plants like deadly nightshade, bracken, and ragwort may poison a horse if it eats even a small quantity. Pastures where horses are left to graze must be cleared of these plants.

• Horses should not graze in an area within 14 days of any spraying.

BEHAVIOR

TODAY'S DOMESTIC HORSES show
the same patterns of behavior as
their wild ancestors. The herd
instinct still dominates, and horses
prefer to be kept in groups rather
than on their own. Much of their
behavior is linked to the way they
communicate with other horses.

*Horses sleep
for only short
periods at
a time.*

SLEEPING
Horses are able to sleep
standing up. In the wild
this increases their
chances of escaping
from predators.

EARS
The position of a horse's ears is an
important indicator of its mood. If the
ears point forward, this shows curiosity.
When the horse is uncertain, it keeps one
ear forward and the other backward.

SHIRE HORSE

FLEHMENING
When a mare
is close to a
stallion, the
stallion may
fold back his
lips and draw
air into his
mouth to detect
the mare's scent
to sense if she is
ready to mate. This
action is called
flehmening.

MUTUAL GROOMING
Horses indulge in
mutual grooming as
a sign of a close
relationship. They
will gently nuzzle
each other's back
nibbling at the
hair. Such sessio
may last for sever
minutes at a time

REARING
A stallion rears up to intimidate a rival, often lashing out with his front feet at the same time.

Horse uses its front legs to balance

Horses often rear in play.

ROLLING OVER
By rolling, a horse can exercise the muscles in its back, and also clean its coat. Horses often roll when turned out to graze in a field.

Stallions rear naturally in the wild.

Horses nuzzle each other to establish their relationship.

SHETLAND PONY

BEHAVIORAL FACTS
• Horses will call out to warn others of approaching danger.

• The tail is used as a fly swish rather than for communication.

• Repeated pawing at the ground with the hooves is often a sign of nervousness.

• A horse's ears are very mobile and can rotate independently in a full circle.

LIFE CYCLE OF A HORSE

MARES NEED ONLY BE three or four years old before they are ready to give birth. After mating, it is almost a year before the foal is born and it takes another five before it becomes a fully grown adult horse. Most horses have a life span of around 25 years.

Early development

A mare is ready to mate at intervals of roughly three weeks from spring to autumn. During these intervals, which last five to seven days, she is said to be in heat and will be ready to accept an approach by a stallion.

MATING
When a mare is in heat, her behavior changes and she often seeks the company of other horses more than is usual.

Stallions have to be careful when they approach mares, as the mare may kick out

DEVELOPMENT FACTS

• Male foals usually spend more time in the womb than females.

• It is not obvious that a mare is pregnant until after five months.

• The mare's belly drops before she is ready to give birth.

• Mares can give birth at two years old, but this is unusual.

• It is rare for a horse to give birth to twins.

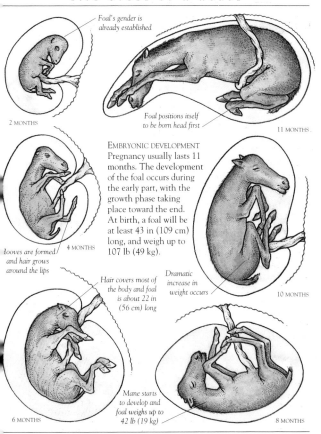

Foal's gender is already established

2 MONTHS

Foal positions itself to be born head first

11 MONTHS

Iooves are formed and hair grows around the lips

4 MONTHS

EMBRYONIC DEVELOPMENT
Pregnancy usually lasts 11 months. The development of the foal occurs during the early part, with the growth phase taking place toward the end. At birth, a foal will be at least 43 in (109 cm) long, and weigh up to 107 lb (49 kg).

Dramatic increase in weight occurs

10 MONTHS

Hair covers most of the body and foal is about 22 in (56 cm) long

Mane starts to develop and foal weighs up to 42 lb (19 kg)

6 MONTHS

8 MONTHS

Growing up

The usual time for a foal to be born is during early summer, when grass and other food is most plentiful, to help the mare's milk supply. Horses develop quickly from young foals into adults. A horse can be independent of its mother by the time it is six months old reaching full adult size between the ages of four and five years. It is at its strongest between the ages of five and 15.

Mare licks foal clean.

Foals take milk at frequent intervals.

Legs are long in proportion to the body

Large eyes

1 NEWBORN
A new foal can stand on its feet within half an hour of its birth. It is carefully watched over by its mother.

2 TWO WEEKS
After two weeks, the foal is used to walking. To give it extra stability, it stands with its rear legs slightly apart, as it cannot yet straighten its legs. The hooves are small and soft. The tail is short and bushy, while the mane stands up on its neck and is light and feathery.

3 FIVE WEEKS
At five weeks, the foal still has a soft woolly coat, known as milk hair. The upper bones of its legs become longer, and the foal can now stand upright.

4 EIGHT WEEKS
The foal lives solely on its mother's milk for its first two months, after which it gradually begins to eat grass, until it is fully weaned at around six months old. After two months, the foal's fluffy milk hair begins to be shed and is replaced by its adult coat.

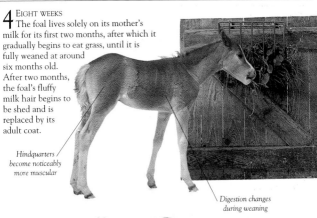

Hindquarters become noticeably more muscular

Digestion changes during weaning

Muscles become firmer

5 FOUR MONTHS
The foal's body has grown to adult proportions. The neck and tail have lengthened, and the legs continue to become stronger as their muscles develop further. The hooves also become harder.

GROWING-UP FACTS

• As soon as they are born, new foals shiver to maintain their body temperature.

• The mother's first milk, called colostrum, contains antibodies, which protect the foal against infections.

• After weaning, horse breeders usually give foals a concentrated feed with supplements to ensure that the foals grow healthy.

USES OF THE HORSE

IN SPITE OF THE SPREAD of mechanization, the horse still has a place in society. Today, horses can be found at work in cities, forests, and farmland. While traditional horse sports, like racing and steeple-chasing remain popular, they are now being joined by leisure activities such as trail riding.

Working horses

Horses work in forests because they cause less damage than tractors. Farmers in developing countries also find horses easy to keep, as they can live off the land. Though no longer used in war, horses are retained in many countries for ceremonial duties and the police horse has so far proved irreplaceable.

MULE TRAINS
Even in the late 20th century, it has been hard to find anything to replace the mule to transport goods over uneven ground. Mules are still used in India, China, and Southeast Asia.

London police horses undergo about 40 weeks of training.

ROYAL
ARTILLERY
HORSE AND
RIDER

CEREMONIAL DUTIES

Many countries still use horses for ceremonial duties. This dates from wars where horses were used as cavalry and to haul artillery.

POLICE HORSES

Mounted police can be seen in many cities today. Horses offer the rider a good view and mobility, and can move through crowds more easily than either motorcycles or cars.

WORKING HORSE FACTS

• More horses are bred in the United States for leisure riding than for herding cattle.

• India employs more mounted police than any other country in the world.

• Heavy horses are used in Canadian forests to pull up trees and take them away and to cultivate the soil afterward.

Working cow ponies in the US tend to average 15 hh.

QUARTER
HORSE

Average working life of a police horse is about 14 years.

BRITISH POLICE
HORSES AND
RIDERS IN
CEREMONIAL
DRESS

HERDING CATTLE

People first used the horse to herd sheep and cattle over 6,000 years ago and still do so in North America and Australia.

Horses for sport and leisure

Since the end of World War II, there has been a tremendous increase in the use of the horse for pleasure. The sport of horse racing remains as popular as ever, and interest in such competition as show jumping and dressage has been heightened by television. Riding vacations are now a popular and relaxing pastime for many people.

POLO
Probably originating in Persia, polo has been played for 2,500 years. Modern polo is played by two teams of four using long mallets to hit the ball into the opposition's goal.

DRESSAGE
The American Morgan Horse, once favored by the US cavalry, is shown in ridden and harnessed classes. It is also used for Western and pleasure riding, and jumping.

Rider sits on the horse's center of balance

A hard hat protects the rider's head in case of a fall

Pony will cover 3–6 miles (4.8–6.4 km) in an hour

The use of plain snaffle bridles for recreational riding is almost universal

RACEHORSES
Horse racing has become a huge international industry. This statue in the Kentucky Horse Park is of the famous racehorse *Man O' War*, or *Big Red*, who was beaten only once in 21 races. When he died in 1947, more than 1,000 people attended his funeral.

HORSE SPORTS FACTS

• The longest-running horse race is the Palio in Siena, Italy, begun in the 1200s and still run today. The winning horse attends a special banquet afterward.

• The word polo comes from the Tibetan *pulu*, meaning ball.

• The first steeplechase was held in 1830 in St. Albans, England.

Riders learn to use aids such as the reins

Each rider keeps a pony-length away from the next

A novice rider is given a quiet, reliable horse

Riding school ponies are frequently cross-bred animals

RIDING VACATIONS
Those who want to ride occasionally or just for pleasure, can take a riding vacation. These rides can last from a single day to a whole week. The distance covered in each day varies between 10–25 miles (16–40 km). Trips are always supervised and provide an opportunity to reach beautiful and inaccessible areas of a country.

HORSEBACK RIDING

PEOPLE HAVE RIDDEN HORSES for many different reasons. Even before the invention of the wheel, horses provided fast transportation. Soldiers rode horses during wartime and explorers often traveled on horseback over unknown territory.

Riding styles

One of the oldest schools of riding is that of the Iberian Peninsula in Portugal and Spain. The techniques and swift movements originate with cattle herding and the practice of mounted bullfighting.

High saddle provides security

An Army Universal Pelham used here as a curbed bit

Flat metal stirrup

SPANISH RIDING
Spain and Portugal use such breeds as Andalucian, Lusitano, and Alter-Real to perform High School equitation that is linked, nonetheless, to the requirements of the bullring.

WESTERN RIDING
This style was derived from the Spanish settlers and adapted by American cowboys who virtually lived in the saddle. The Western style involves a longer leather and the Western jog makes rising (or posting) to the trot unnecessary.

The Western horse can be trained in a bitless Hackamore bridle

Apron has a heavy hem to stop it from flying around

CLASSICAL RIDING SCHOOL
Riding as a trained skill was first made popular in Italy in the 16th century.

SIDESADDLE
Sometimes called the "Saddle of Queens," sidesaddle riding was first seen over 600 years ago in the courts of Europe. It was soon considered unladylike to ride astride.

LIPIZZANER WITH SIDESADDLE RIDER

RIDING STYLE FACTS
• Classical riding of the Renaissance was based on the Spanish horse of the period.

• Women rode astride until the 15th century.

• In classical riding, the horse's leaps or kicks are called "airs."

Equipment

In the early days, horses were ridden either bareback or with a simple cloth pad and were guided by a rope attached to their lower jaw. It was only during the late Roman period that saddles were used for the first time. Stirrups were probably introduced to Europe by the Huns under Attila in the 5th century.

BIT
This long-cheeked curb bit dates from the 16th century. It has a shaped mouthpiece that allows room for the horse's tongue

Rowel pricks the horse's side

BRASS ROWEL SPUR FROM SOUTH AMERICA, c.1800

Buckle attaches spur to boot

MOTIVATION
Spurs are used to urge a horse to go forward. In the past, some particularly cruel spurs were devised which cut into the horse's side, but today they never have sharp edges.

Chinese slipper stirrup, 11th century

LEG AID
Stirrups support the rider, enabling long distances to be covered comfortably. When riding at speed, a shorter stirrup leather is used, as in the case of race riding.

SADDLE
This is the type of saddle used in the classical schools of the 18th century. It was called *Selle à Piquer*.

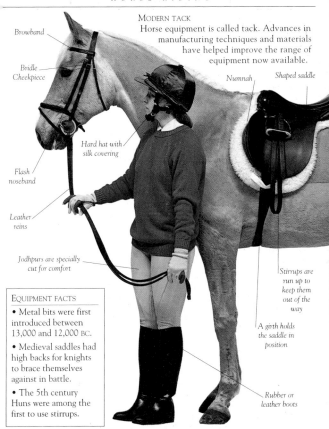

MODERN TACK

Horse equipment is called tack. Advances in manufacturing techniques and materials have helped improve the range of equipment now available.

Browband

Bridle Cheekpiece

Numnah

Shaped saddle

Hard hat with silk covering

Flash noseband

Leather reins

Jodhpurs are specially cut for comfort

Stirrups are run up to keep them out of the way

A girth holds the saddle in position

Rubber or leather boots

EQUIPMENT FACTS

• Metal bits were first introduced between 13,000 and 12,000 BC.

• Medieval saddles had high backs for knights to brace themselves against in battle.

• The 5th century Huns were among the first to use stirrups.

PONIES

INTRODUCTION TO PONIES

PONIES HAVE BEEN AROUND ever since the equine species evolved. They belong, of course, to the genus *Equus* but are distinguished from today's horses by particular characteristics. Ponies are smaller, no taller than 14.2 hands high, with shorter legs in relation to their height. They also live longer and are hardier.

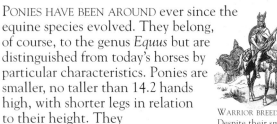

WARRIOR BREED
Despite their small size, ponies were used as war horses by European warriors such as Vikings

PONY POWER
In the past, ponies provided a means of transportation. Stronger for their size than horses, ponies were able to pull traps (small carts) without difficulty. Ponies are now popular for use in driving competitions.

Thick tail keeps out the cold

Wooden spoked wheels

19TH-CENTURY
LIVERPOOL
PONY GIG

Strong hind-
quarters

Head is
similar to a
Thoroughbred's

Limbs and joints
must be strong
and well-formed

POLO PONY
This is not a breed, but a type of pony
produced for a particular purpose. Polo
demands that the animal must be fast and surefooted. So, the first polo ponies were bred by
crossing Thoroughbreds for speed, and ponies
for stability.

Short, powerful
limbs with
strong bones

Hard feet,
notably free
from disease

HARD HOOF
Ponies are more surefooted than
horses. They have particularly
tough hooves and seldom go lame.
These characteristics are derived
from their former mountain and
moorland environment.

SHETLAND

THESE PONIES WERE named after the bleak Shetland Islands off the northeast coast of Scotland, where they have been bred for more than 2,000 years. Their ancestors were either brought over from the mainland or from Scandinavia. In spite of their small size, the Shetlands are a tough and hardy breed.

LARGE AND SMALL
As more people have kept Shetlands, some breeders have developed a smaller pony for use as a pet. This has given rise to the Miniature Shetland which has proved popular.

NATIVE HABITAT
There are no trees on the Shetland Islands to provide firewood, so islanders dug up peat on the moors for fuel. This was carried to their villages by the ponies, which are very strong for their small size.

Weather-resistant coat, double-layered in winter

Muscular neck

Strong, rounded feet

10

THELWELL CARTOON
The Shetland is a good choice for a young rider, but it can get fat if not exercised regularly – as this drawing by the British cartoonist Thelwell shows.

AMERICAN SHETLAND

This modern breed is the result of combining the Shetland primarily with Hackney blood, and bears no close resemblance to its island ancestor. The American pony is slimmer and has a more refined look.

Hair of mane and tail is thin and usually soft

RIDING PONY
Although the Shetland is probably more suited to harness, it can be used as a first riding pony for small children. It is very surefooted and thrives on a minimum feed ration.

Long-haired tail, especially full to protect against the weather

Back legs are strong and firm

HIGHLAND

THE LARGEST AND STRONGEST of Britain's ponies is the Highland. Originally small, the size and strength of these ponies was increased by crossings with Percheron heavy horses in the 16th century. Later, Arab input made them more suitable for riding. Today's Highland combines strength with an easygoing nature.

Wide forehead combined with short head

Neck is strong and arched

Broad, wide nostrils

Strong forelegs with large flat knees

Long h is soft c silky

CAVE PAINTINGS
This painting from cave walls at Lascaux, France, dates back about 14,000 years to the end of the last Ice Age. Some of these drawings bear a striking resemblance to the modern dun-colored Highland.

Pony reckoned to be about 13 hh

Western Isles
SCOTLAND
IRELAND
ENGLAND

HIGHLAND HOMELAND
Ponies have lived in the upland areas of northern Scotland and on some of the nearby Western Isles for more than 10,000 years. They are still used in the forest, for trekking, and in harness.

COLORED COATS
Highlands are bred in many colors. This pony is dun with a black mane and tail, and black lower legs. A dense double-layered coat gives good protection in bad weather conditions.

Short, strong back

Tail set high and has fine, silky texture

Some have zebra-like markings on the lower leg

Hard hooves enable the pony to thrive on rough ground

14

CLYDESDALE INFLUENCE
During the 19th century, the Highland was made bigger and stronger as a result of crossings with the Clydesdale. But the breed's coarser looks were considered to be unattractive.

Longer legs than most heavy breeds

FELL AND DALES

THESE TWO MOORLAND BREEDS descend from a common root. Their early ancestor was the Friesian horse employed by Roman mercenaries guarding Hadrian's Wall (in what is now northern England). Their greatest influence however, is the swift Scottish Galloway of the 17th and 18th centuries. Both breeds are used extensively in harness for trekking.

Long tail trails close to the ground

Massive hind legs provide propulsion

14

TOUGH UPBRINGING
The natural habitat of the Fell and Dales is the rugged, hilly Pennine region of northern England. The Fell developed on the west side and the Dales on the east. The rough countryside has made both ponies hardy breeds, with plenty of stamina. They have hard feet, which do not wear down even when walking long distances over rough tracks. The ponies trot quickly and move freely.

FELL

The Fell is smaller and lighter than the Dales and was once preferred for riding. However, it could also carry heavy loads of 224 lb (102 kg) or more. It was not unusual for a pony to cover 240 miles (384 km) a week.

HACKNEY PONY

As a result of a bloodline developed in the 1880s, which was later crossbred with Trotters and Roadsters, the Fell has added to the ancestry of the Hackney Pony.

The Hackney is the supreme harness horse

Broad, open nostrils

DALES

In the past, the heavier-built Dales were valued as pack ponies. They carried lead ore mined on the moors to the ports of northeastern England.

Strong hindquarters

Broad, sloping shoulders

Tough blue horn hooves, with hair at the heels

14.2

Deep girth, with long and rounded ribs

EXMOOR AND DARTMOOR

NAMED AFTER THEIR moorland habitats, both these ponies come from southwestern England. The Exmoor is the oldest British breed of pony and its ancestors may have roamed over Exmoor before the Bronze Age, about 4,000 years ago. The younger Dartmoor dates back 1,000 years, but today's pony looks little like it did then.

WORKING PONY
Like most ponies, the Exmoor and Dartmoor have been used as pack animals. The Dartmoor used to carry tin from mines on the moor to nearby towns.

Mottled coloring on muzzle and around the eyes

EXMOOR PONY
These ponies have had to adapt to survive hrsh Exmoor winters. A fan-like area of hair at the top of their tail prevents water from penetrating and then freezing. Long nasal passages allow cold air to be warmed as it is inhaled.

Compact body with long ribs and deep chest

Thick, springy coat provides warmth in winter

Short legs and neat hooves

12

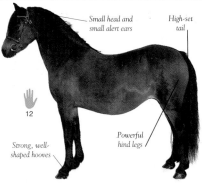

Small head and small alert ears

High-set tail

12

Powerful hind legs

Strong, well-shaped hooves

EXMOOR PONY FACTS

• The eyes of the Exmoor pony are called "toad eyes," and are hooded to protect them from the rain and snow.

• The ponies dislike dogs, possibly because of an ancestral fear of wolves which used to live on Exmoor.

• Purebred Exmoors are marked with a star-shaped brand on their left shoulder, with their herd number beneath.

DARTMOOR PONY

As a result of crossings with other breeds, the modern Dartmoor is a particularly elegant-looking pony. It does not lift its knees as high as other ponies, and has a better riding action as a result.

HARSH HABITAT

Dartmoor, in the English county of Devon, is crossed by the Dart, Tavy, and Taw rivers. Conditions here can be tough, and the ponies had to be hardy and surefooted to thrive. Today, few of these ponies are still to be seen on the moors.

NEW FOREST PONY

FOR MORE THAN a thousand years, these hardy little ponies have roamed the New Forest in southern England. Oddly, the "forest" is mainly a large expanse of moorland covered with heather. Ponies have only been allowed to stay in the forest throughout the year since 1877. Until then, it was thought that there was not enough food for them. Even today, the herd is limited to 2,500 to prevent overgrazing.

Large head reflects the influence of other horse breeds

NEW FOREST FACTS

• The New Forest Pony is the second largest of the British Mountain and Moorland ponies.

• The ponies feed on prickly shrubs in winter. In spring, they must be watched to stop them from wandering into boggy ground, where the first shoots of grass appear.

• Speeding vehicles injure or kill about 100 ponies every year.

NEW FOREST GUARDIANS

The ponies are owned by Commoners – people who have the right to graze their stock inside the forest. Four wardens, called Agisters, organize a roundup of the animals in late summer to check for any health problems and deal with any emergencies.

PONY AUCTION
Each year some of the
ponies are sold by
auction. Their friendly
nature means they are in
great demand for
young riders and
for driving.

*Can be any
color except
pinto or
albino.*

*Straight,
powerful legs
and hard,
round hooves*

IMPROVING THE BREED
The New Forest Ponies
have been purebred for
only 50 years. Many
breeds have played a part
in their history. Once, an
Arabian stallion called
Zorah, owned by Queen
Victoria, was released into
the forest in an attempt to
breed with the ponies and
improve their appearance.

13

WELSH MOUNTAIN PONY AND AUSTRALIAN PONY

PONIES CAN BE related to each other, even if they live on opposite sides of the world. The Welsh Mountain Pony is the smallest and oldest of four Welsh breeds. In the early 19th century, many Welsh ponies were exported to Australia, where they played an important part in the development of the Australian Pony.

Large eyes

Wide nostrils

WELSH MOUNTAIN PONY
In the 18th century, the breed was influenced by a Thoroughbred called *Merlin*. In Wales, a pony is still called a "merlin".

PONIES OF THE VALLEY
Welsh Mountain Ponies still roam the Welsh valleys in some numbers.

Short, stocky body with a deep chest

Hooves are made of blue horn, which is sound and hard

12

AUSTRALIAN PONY

This breed still has a strong resemblance to its Welsh relative and can be any solid color. It is highly valued as a riding pony in Australia, where horse sports are very popular.

Neat head with long, crested neck shows Arab influence

12–14

A distinct type was established by the late 1920s

Sloping shoulders give the ponies a long stride and smooth action

VARIED MIXTURE

The early settlers of Australia brought a variety of breeds with them and the Australian Pony was developed from these.

WELSH PONY FACTS

• Welsh Mountain Ponies have many attractive features, including small, pointed ears, and large, luminous eyes.

• The earliest records of these ponies date back to Roman times.

• Most of the ponies are gray, but some are bay, chestnut, or palomino.

• The ponies can survive on the sparse, reedy moorland grasses.

CONNEMARA

THE ONLY NATIVE Irish pony is the Connemara. Its ancestors probably resembled the ponies of Shetland, Iceland, and Norway, but in the 16th century Galway merchants introduced Spanish and Barb horses into Ireland. These interbred to produce the Irish Hobby, forerunner of the Connemara. The modern Connemara is an all-round performance pony.

CONNEMARA COUNTRY
The pony is named after the area of Connemara, which is part of County Galway, on the north-western coast of Ireland.

CONNEMARA FACTS

• Connemaras are long-lived, very strong and hardy, and notably free from disease.

• The first registered Connemara stallion, Cannon Ball, won the annual farmers' race at Oughterard, Ireland, for 16 successive years.

• In Galway, this pony was used on farms and as a pack animal to carry seaweed, potatoes, peat, and corn.

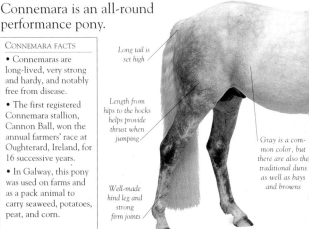

Long tail is set high

Length from hips to the hocks helps provide thrust when jumping

Gray is a common color, but there are also the traditional duns as well as bays and browns

Well-made hind leg and strong firm joints

OD AND SIZE
n the boggy ground of
eir Irish homeland,
onnemaras exist on a
et of sparse grass. They
ually grow to a larger
e when given richer
od. Connemaras are
en crossed with
oroughbreds to produce
mpetition horses.

WELSH COB INFLUENCE

In the 19th century, many Irish farmers were very poor and as a result, the Connemaras also suffered. Welsh Cobs from Britain were introduced to improve the stock.

Small, neat head shows Arab influence

HOMELAND HABITAT

The native environment of the Connemara is a wild, isolated expanse of marshes, lakes, and mountains. The ponies have been working on farms in this area for centuries.

Long neck and sloping shoulders show the pony is good for riding

14

CHINCOTEAGUE

A BOOK AND A FILM have made this delightful little pony part of the childhood of many Americans. The Chincoteague lives on two islands off the eastern coast of the US. It is said to be descended from horses that survived a shipwreck close to the coast and swam ashore.

Large head compared to the rest of the body

Heavy shoulders and straight forelimbs

HORSELIKE PONY
It is likely that Spanish blood was originally involved in the ancestry of the Chincoteague, but poor grazing and possibly inbreeding have resulted in a reduction in its size. As a result, it resembles a small horse rather than a pony.

Cannons are long and joints often poorly developed

12

Condition of the feet may vary

ISLAND HOME
The current population of around 200 Chincoteagues lives mostly on the island of Assateague, now a national park. The ponies are rounded up at the end of July for the annual sale, and made to swim across the channel to Chincoteague. Any ponies that are not sold return by the same route the following day.

CHINCOTEAGUE FACTS

• The Native American meaning of Chincoteague is "beautiful land across the waters."

• The existence of the ponies became generally known only in the 1920s.

• The ponies were made famous by the 1947 children's book entitled *Misty of Chincoteague* and a film made in 1961.

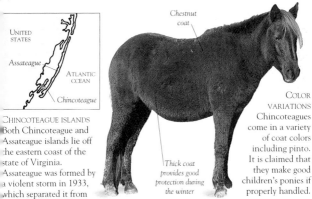

Chestnut coat

UNITED STATES

Assateague

ATLANTIC OCEAN

Chincoteague

CHINCOTEAGUE ISLANDS
Both Chincoteague and Assateague islands lie off the eastern coast of the state of Virginia. Assateague was formed by a violent storm in 1933, which separated it from the mainland.

Thick coat provides good protection during the winter

COLOR VARIATIONS
Chincoteagues come in a variety of coat colors including pinto. It is claimed that they make good children's ponies if properly handled.

HAFLINGER

THIS AUSTRIAN pony originates from the village of Hafling in the Etschlander Mountains. It is descended from other local ponies, the Arabian, and extinct Alpine Heavy Horse breeds. A true Haflinger is either palomino or chestnut in color, with a flaxen mane and tail. It may be harnessed or ridden.

Flowing flaxen tail is thick and full.

Noriker's ancestors were bred by the Romans.

Broad and compact body with a deep girth

HAFLINGER FACTS

• The young foals are brought up on the Alpine fields, where their lungs develop in the thin air.

• In Austria, Haflingers are not worked until they are four years old.

• They may live for more than 40 years.

NORIKER

Half of all horses in Austria are Norikers. The ancestors of this native Austrian breed were bred by the Romans for draft and pack work. Today, it is still a working horse and can be seen near the central Alpine region, adjacent to the Austrian Tyrol, home of the Haflinger.

EDELWEISS BRAND

FLOWER BRAND
The Haflinger is also
called the Edelweiss
Pony because its brand
is the shape of
Austria's national
flower.

*Striking mane and
small, elegant head
reflect Arabian blood.*

Large
eyes

Big nostrils

13

HAFLINGER
This pony is powerfully
built, with well-made legs
and sloping shoulders. The
long back reflects its use as a
packpony. The ponies are
surefooted with a long stride,
even when walking across
steep mountainous terrain.

IN THE MOUNTAINS
In its native Austria,
Haflingers are harnessed to
sleighs as a means of
transportation in thick snow.
Many are kept for use in the
tourist season, when they
pull old-fashioned carriages.

CASPIAN

THOUGHT TO HAVE BEEN EXTINCT for more than a thousand years, the Caspian was rediscovered in Iran in 1965. A small herd was established at Nourouzabad by Mrs. Louise L. Firouz. Caspian societies and studs now exist in North and South America, UK and Australia.

A Caspian has one more molar than other horses

CASPIAN FACTS

• The ancient Greeks found feral horses on the edge of the Caspian Sea 2500 years ago.

• Twenty Caspians found in 1970 were used to start the Nourouzabad stud near Teheran, Iran.

• Apart from the Asiatic wild horse, the Caspian is the oldest surviving breed.

MINIATURE HORSE
The Caspian is usually described as a miniature horse rather than a pony. It has a short head, covered with the fine, thin skin of desert breeds, and large eyes and nostrils. The ears are very short and should not exceed 4.5 in (11 cm).

Shoulders slope like a horse's, giving a longer stride than true ponies

11

Strong, oval-shaped feet never need shoeing

AREA OF DISCOVERY
The pony is named after the Caspian Sea, on the border of Iran.

MOUNTAIN HOME
Caspians live in a remote part of Iran where there is little rain and the temperature can vary widely. The area is cut off from the rest of the country by the Elburz mountains. This meant that the ponies did not mix with other breeds and remained pure.

EGYPTIAN CARVING

CASPIAN ANCESTOR
The ancestor of the Caspian is thought to be the smallest of the four main types of horses from which all the main horse breeds developed. This type, simply called Horse Type 4, lived in western Asia and was probably no more than 9 hh. Miniature horses similar to the Caspian have been found on Eygptian artifacts 3,500 years old.

Tail is carried high, as on the Arab

FALABELLA

THE SMALLEST BREED of horse in the world, the Falabella is named after the Argentine family who developed it. Although its size suggests it is a pony, its proportions make it closer to a small horse. The Falabella is generally kept as a pet, being unsuitable for all but the very youngest rider. These little horses may also be seen in the show ring, often pulling scaled-down carts.

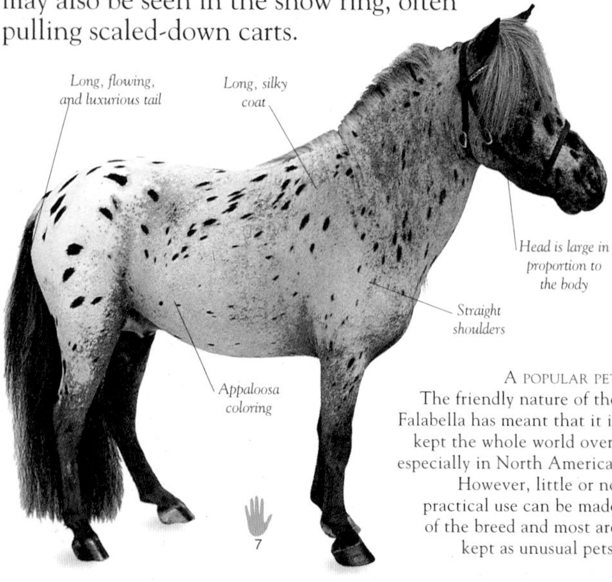

Long, flowing, and luxurious tail

Long, silky coat

Head is large in proportion to the body

Straight shoulders

Appaloosa coloring

7

A POPULAR PET
The friendly nature of the Falabella has meant that it is kept the whole world over, especially in North America. However, little or no practical use can be made of the breed and most are kept as unusual pets.

SPECIAL SIZE

The size of the Falabella was achieved by intense inbreeding of the smallest specimen, a practise that can result in serious genetic weaknesses. However, now that the breed is well established, breeders try to mate unrelated Falabellas when breeding.

Legs may be weak and cow hocks are often in evidence

FALABELLA FACTS

• Miniature horses were first recorded in ancient China from 206 BC.

• Newborn Falabellas are tiny, standing about 5 hh, and weighing around 15 lb (7 kg).

• The smallest example bred by Julio Falabella was a mare barely 4 hh and weighing just over 26 lb (12 kg).

• Falabellas can pull 20 times their own weight.

SOUTH AMERICA

Buenos Aires

PLACE OF DEVELOPMENT

In 1860, an Irishman called Newton attempted to perfect the shape of two miniature South American horses. This was later achieved by his grandson, Julio Cesar Falabella, at the family ranch close to Buenos Aires in South America.

COLORS AND PATTERNS

Color can be a factor contributing to the value of the Falabella. Today, there is a wide range of colors, and both solid and part colors are acceptable. Above all, the spotted Appaloosa pattern is particularly popular.

Bay coat

Chestnut coat

ICELANDIC HORSE

IN SPITE OF ITS SMALL SIZE, this animal is described as a horse rather than a pony. Originating from Norway, the Icelandic Horse has not been crossed with any other breed for more than 1,000 years and looks much like it did in the days of the Vikings. These historic horses are still used in Iceland for transportation, farm work, and sports.

Neck carries long, thick mane

Head is large and heavy compared with the body

BARREN LANDSCAPE
The Icelandic Horse still roams across Iceland's barren landscape. It is a hardy breed, able to survive outdoors in the bitter cold of the northern winter.

GREENLAND SEA

ICELAND

ICELANDIC SETTLERS
Horses were taken to
Iceland between 935 BC
and AD 860. A hundred
years later, the Icelandic
parliament made it illegal
to import other breeds so
as to keep the Icelandic
Horse pure.

ICELANDIC FACTS

• Norsemen made
their horses fight
each other for sport.

• The Icelandic Horse
can be bred in up to
15 different colors.

• These horses have
taken part in races in
Iceland since 1874.

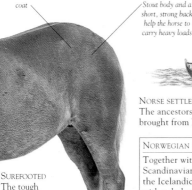

Chestnut
coat

Stout body and a
short, strong back
help the horse to
carry heavy loads

NORSE SETTLERS
The ancestors of the Icelandic Horse were
brought from Norway in Norse long boats.

NORWEGIAN FJORD INFLUENCE

Together with the Tarpan, this
Scandinavian pony formed the basis of
the Icelandic Horse. It is dun in color
with a dark stripe running
from its forelock to
the tip of
its tail.

Pony was
formerly
called the
Westland

SUREFOOTED
The tough
Icelandic horse is
exceptionally
surefooted and
crosses rough
ground easily.

13–14

LIGHT HORSES

INTRODUCTION TO LIGHT HORSES

THE LEAN AND athletic light horse is fast and comfortable to ride. This is because of the shape of its body, with sloping shoulders and a back ideally suited to carrying a saddle. Once popular as a cavalry mount or for pulling coaches, today's light horses are used mostly for pleasure. Many modern breeds have been developed for this purpose.

Deep, compact body shape

COLORADO RANGER

COAT PATTERNS
Light horses come in a variety of colors and patterns – more so than ponies or heavy horses. The Colorado Ranger is a spotted breed. Its pattern is purely decorative and did not develop as camouflage.

LIGHT HORSE FACTS
• Some horses are famously hardy. In 1935, a group of Akhal Teke horses survived a ride of 600 miles (966 km) across the desert with little water.

• The vast herds of North American horses stemmed from 11 stallions and five mares brought over by Spanish conquistadors.

ORLOV TROTTER
This elegant breed was developed by Count Alexis Orlov in the 18th century. It is still raced in harness but is not as fast as the American Standardbred.

CATTLE HORSES

The cowboy and his horse have long been synonymous with the North American West. The speed and agility of light horses made them well suited to rounding up sheep and cattle. Their endurance meant that they could cope with long trail rides.

Chaps protect the cowboy's legs from thorns

Palomino has a golden coat with a white mane and tail

Western bridle with curbed bit is of Spanish origin

SHAGYA ARAB

Some light horses were developed at breeding centers. The Shagya Arab comes from this stud farm at Babolna, Hungary. Early on, an Arab stallion called *Shagya* was involved in the breeding, giving the horses their name.

BARB

THE ANCESTORS OF this ancient horse were living in North Africa as far back as the last ice age. The Barb was taken to Europe by the Moors in the 7th century. Some remained when the Moors left in the early 700s and played a vital role in the development of today's breeds.

HEAD DETAIL
The wide muzzle is nearly as broad as the forehead. The narrow skull is similar to the early primitive types such as Przewalski's Horse.

Head is long and nose can be curved.

Curved neck is covered by long flowing mane.

Shoulders are flat and upright.

Deep girth and short, strong back give the breed its stamina.

BARB FACTS

• The Barb was used in battle for centuries and is still ridden by Berber tribes of North Africa.

• Traditionally, Barbs are bay, dark bay, or black in color. Gray was introduced after crossings with Arabians.

• More than a dozen of today's breeds have Barb blood in their ancestries.

MASTER OF THE DESERT
The Barb is renowned for its endurance and copes well with heat and drought. It is not a race-horse, but is fast over short distances. The Barb has Arabian blood, and although there are similarities, the Barb has a heavier build.

15

Arched neck is
carried proudly.

Strong
shoulders

Hooves
of tough
blue horn

COUNTRY OF ORIGIN
The Barb originally came
from the Barbary coast in
northwest Africa – hence
the name.

FRIESIAN
Evidence of the Barb's stamina and good
character can be found in its relative, the
Dutch Friesian. The black color and stylish
movement of this breed made it
a popular choice for pulling
hearses in Europe during
the 19th century.

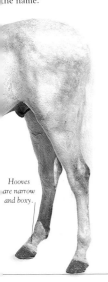

Hooves
are narrow
and boxy.

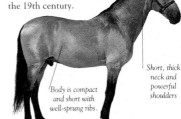

Short, thick
neck and
powerful
shoulders

Body is compact
and short with
well-sprung ribs.

LUSITANO
The Portuguese Lusitano was developed as a
cavalry and coach horse during the 1500s. It
inherited its agility from the Barb and still puts
this to good use in the bullring.

THOROUGHBRED

THE FASTEST HORSE in the world is the Thoroughbred, and it is unlikely that a faster breed will ever be produced. This horse was developed in England during the 17th and 18th centuries especially for the sport of horse racing. Today, the Thoroughbred is at the center of a huge international industry and is bred in over 50 countries. It is also a major influence on many other competition breeds.

STUD FARMING
The first Thoroughbreds were produced when British running horses owned by the royal family were crossed with stallions from Turkey and Arabia. Thoroughbred stud farms have been around for over 200 years, and some stallions are worth a small fortune.

Powerful hindquarters

Long hind legs

Hard feet

QUICK COMPETITOR

Thoroughbreds start to race when only two years old, and most retire after about two years. They compete on flat ground or over fences, and can reach a speed of 40 mph (60 km/h). The first modern racecourse was set up in the 17th century near the English village of Newmarket.

UNIVERSAL APPEAL

All modern Thoroughbreds are descended from three stallions living in the mid-1700s. But it is only in the last 100 years that the breed has established its worldwide appeal.

Long, sloping shoulders help its easy galloping movement

Deep girth gives good lung capacity

Coat is fine and silky

Large joints

16

DUTCH WARMBLOOD

This breed of sports horse was developed in the Netherlands as recently as the 1960s. It is partly derived from the Thoroughbred, and careful breeding has made it a horse of the highest quality. Many are used for dressage.

Good muscle tone

PINTO AND PALOMINO

SOME HORSES are recognized as a breed because of their coloring. This is the case of the Pinto and Palomino which are strictly color types and not true breeds. The Palomino, has a distinctive golden coloring, while the two-colored coat of the Pinto is associated with many other horse and pony breeds. Both horses are much in demand for western trail rides.

RIDER AND PINTO

FAVORITE MOUNT
The Pinto's camouflage coat made it a favorite mount of the Native Americans.

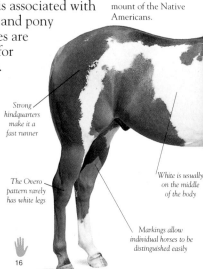

Strong hindquarters make it a fast runner

White is usually on the middle of the body

The Overo pattern rarely has white legs

Markings allow individual horses to be distinguished easily

PALOMINO FACTS

• The Palomino is descended from the Spanish horses brought to the US by settlers in the 1500s.

• The name Palomino originates from Juan de Palomino, the Spanish Don, who was given a horse of this color.

• In Spain, the color palomino is sometimes called Ysabella after a queen who liked it.

16

PALOMINO COLORING
The correct coloring is vital for a Palomino to be registered with the Palomino Horse Association. Its coat is the gold of a newly minted gold coin, and can be only three shades lighter or darker. Mane and tail must be white.

Silvery white mane

Body shape influenced by Spanish ancestry

16

Thoroughbred influence is visible in the shape of the head

PINTO COLORING
The name Pinto comes from the Spanish *pintado* (painted). There are two color patterns, Overo and Tobiano: Overo is a colored coat with splashes of white, Tobiano a white coat with large patches of solid color. The native Sioux and Crow nations valued the Pinto for its color and hardiness.

PALOMINO FEATURES
The tail of a Palomino must be white and full. There should be no evidence of a dorsal stripe running down the back. White markings, which are often seen on the legs, must not extend above the knees, or hocks.

Full-length silvery white tail

ARAB

FIERY AND COURAGEOUS, the Arab is not only the purest of today's light horses, but it is also the oldest, having been bred for thousands of years. It has influenced most other horse breeds, especially the Thoroughbred.

Small ears are sometimes turned inwards

ELEGANT ARAB

The Arab has an elegant appearance, with a short head and dished face. Between the eyes is a shield-shaped bulge called the "jibbah". The skin around the muzzle is particularly soft. The large nostrils help the horse to breathe easily when it is running fast.

Curved neck allows the head to turn freely

Tendons are clearly defined

15

BEDOUINS AND THEIR HORSES

Bedouin Arabs have always been closely associated with this "desert horse," which they tamed and introduced into Europe during the 7th century.

BORN IN A LEGEND
Bedouin legend traces the Arab back to a stallion called Hoshaba. He was mated with a mare called Baz, who was said to have been captured by Bax, the great-great-grandson of Noah. Notes on breeding and feeding these horses can be found in the Koran.

COSSACK RIDER

ARAB FACTS

• Napoleon rode his gray Arab *Marengo* into his final battle at Waterloo in 1815.

• In the desert, these horses will eat locusts, meat, and dried dates.

• During the Crimean War of 1851–4, one Arab horse raced 93 miles (150 km) with no ill effects, but the rider died from exhaustion.

• The anatomy of the Arab is unique, as it has fewer vertebrae than other horses.

Tail is set high and arches up behind the body

Back is short and slightly curved

Slim, powerful legs and sound hooves

ENDURANCE HORSE
The Arab is famed for its powers of endurance. In the 1800s, it was not unknown for desert races to last for three days. The Arab's stamina has made it a popular choice for the growing sport of endurance, trail, and long-distance riding.

ARAB WITH SADDLE

QUARTER HORSE

THE FIRST ALL-AMERICAN horse, the Quarter Horse is not named for its well-muscled quarters. Instead, it got its name by racing over quarter-mile (400 m) distances, often down the main street of a town. Developed by the early New World settlers, it is still used on farms.

QUARTER HORSE FACTS
• The founder of the breed was an English Thoroughbred, kept in Virginia between 1756 and 1780.
• Quarter Horses still race in quarter-mile events, such as the All-American Futurity.

COLOR VARIATION
The colour of the Quarter Horse is influenced by its Spanish and Barb ancestors. They can be bred in any solid color, but most are chestnut. The horse below is a bay.

Heavily muscled thighs

Hind leg is perfectly formed

Underside of horse is longer than the back

STRONG QUARTERS
Its powerful, massive quarters help the horse to sprint almost immediately from standing and increase its speed quickly.

Hard, well-formed joints

14

WORKING HORSE

Roping cattle, whether on the range or competing in a rodeo, is dangerous and requires a sturdy mount. Quarter Horses are often used, since they are steady and work well under pressure. They are very agile horses and possess an almost instinctive ability to follow the twists and turns of a particular cow in a herd. This enables a rider to sit securely while concentrating on roping the target animal.

The shape of the back helps to hold the saddle firmly in place

Short, wide head

Small, very refined muzzle

Wide jawbones do not restrict breathing

...ctly
...isterns

MAIN FEATURES

The early Quarter Horses were part Thoroughbred and part Spanish. This produced a chunky, muscular look. Later, more Thoroughbred blood was used to make the breed faster and has given today's Quarter Horse a leaner appearance.

BUCKING BRONCO

A brave rodeo rider tries to hang on to an unbroken horse for as long as possible.

APPALOOSA

ONCE ALMOST EXTINCT, the American Appaloosa is now one of the most numerous horses in the world. It is distinguished by its spotted markings, although these also occur on other breeds. As a cattle horse, it showed its good stamina and easygoing nature. This has encouraged its use for racing and jumping.

HISTORY OF THE BREED

The Appaloosa is descended from spotted Spanish horses brought to America during the 16th century. During the 1700s, it was developed by the Nez Percé tribe of Native Americans in northeastern Oregon. When their territory was taken over by US troops in 1877, the tribe was pursued and the breed nearly wiped out.

Deep body with rounded ribs

APPALOOSA
AND RIDER

Blanket instead of saddle

BLANKET
PATTERN

Tail is short to prevent it from getting caught on desert scrub

Black and white vertical stripes on hooves

15

HEAD DETAIL

An Appaloosa's head is often "hawk"-shaped. The skin on its nose, especially around the nostrils and the lips, is mottled with black and white spots. The white sclera of the eye is a breed characteristic. The registry was started in 1938 and within 50 years had over 400,000 horses.

APPALOOSA FACTS

• This horse was named after the Palouse valley in Oregon.

• Spotted horses were first recorded in Asia and Europe more than 20,000 years ago.

• The earliest known spotted horses came from China.

Sparse, wispy mane with a few short hairs

Sclera of eye visible

Mottling on nose and muzzle

Neck is in proportion to the body

PATTERN VARIATIONS

Appaloosas have five basic coat patterns; three are shown here. A leopard is white with black/brown spots. A snowflake has white spots on a dark body. The blanket is white without dark spots over the hips, a marble is mottled, and a frost has white specks on a dark background.

APPALOOSA CROSSBREED

LEOPARD PATTERN

ANDALUSIAN

ALSO KNOWN AS the Spanish Horse, this breed has had great influence, particularly on the American breeds. Its origins date back to the invasion of Spain in A.D. 711 by the Berber Muslims from North Africa, whose Barb horses mixed with Spanish ponies.

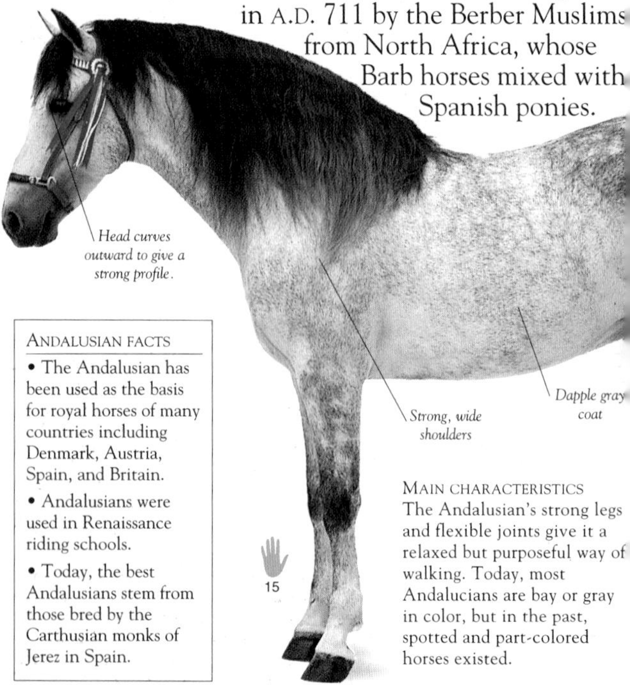
Head curves outward to give a strong profile.
Strong, wide shoulders
Dapple gray coat
15

ANDALUSIAN FACTS

- The Andalusian has been used as the basis for royal horses of many countries including Denmark, Austria, Spain, and Britain.
- Andalusians were used in Renaissance riding schools.
- Today, the best Andalusians stem from those bred by the Carthusian monks of Jerez in Spain.

MAIN CHARACTERISTICS

The Andalusian's strong legs and flexible joints give it a relaxed but purposeful way of walking. Today, most Andalucians are bay or gray in color, but in the past, spotted and part-colored horses existed.

Short, muscular neck is hidden by thick, wavy mane.

SORRAIA PONY INFLUENCE

These native Spanish ponies were mixed with Barbs from North Africa to produce the Andalusian. The hardy Sorraia resists both heat and cold, and was first tamed on the Iberian Peninsula, Europe.

Body shape is similar to that of the ancient Tarpan pony.

MANE POINT

An Andalusian can be recognized by its long, dense, and often wavy mane. This helps to show the neck's highly curved profile.

Decorative flowers

Special harness

SPANISH HORSE FESTIVAL

The home of the Andalusian is in southern Spain, particularly around Jerez de la Frontera, Cordoba, and Seville. Every year there is a horse fair in Jerez in which colorfully decorated horses are paraded through the streets. Andalusians are the traditional mount of the *rejoneadores* (Spanish bullfighters).

CLEVELAND BAY

DESCENDED FROM the Chapman Pack Horses of the Middle Ages, these powerful horses draw royal carriages on state occasions. Bred in the Cleveland area of northeast Yorkshire, they are characterized by a distinctive bay coat with black points, mane, and tail.

Curved and graceful neck

Muscular neck and sloping shoulders provide power

ROYAL CARRIAGE HORSES
The Cleveland Bays used in England to pull the royal carriages are kept in the Royal Mews near Buckingham Palace in London. At one time, the Duke of Edinburgh raced a team of part Cleveland Bays in driving competitions.

16

No feathering on the feet

INFLUENCES

The Cleveland Bay has been influenced by the imports of Spanish and Barb horses brought to the ports of north-east England in the 17th century from Spain and North Africa. It developed into the most powerful and important coach horse of Europe.

BAVARIAN WARMBLOOD

In the late 1700s, Cleveland Bays helped the development of the Bavarian Warmblood, giving it strength and stamina. This German breed is kept as a competition and carriage horse.

Tail is usually black, but gray hairs are a sign of purity

Powerful quarters help the horse to jump well

Legs are characterized by massive bone

CLEVELAND BAY FACTS

• In the Middle Ages, travelling salesmen (chapmen) originally used Clevelands as the Chapman Pack Horse.

• In 1962, Queen Elizabeth II bought and bred one of the last four stallions in order to save the breed from extinction.

• Cleveland Bays have been used as plow and draft horses on farms, as pack horses, and for carrying coal.

TRAKEHNER

ORIGINALLY DEVELOPED to take knights into battle, this horse has a long and colorful history. By the 16th century, the Trakehner was being refined into an elegant coach horse. Its bold and fearless nature made it useful for the cavalry. It is now highly valued in international sporting competitions.

Ears emphasize alert nature

Long elega neck

Face shows horse's similarity to Thoroughbred

Well-balanced body moves very freely

Strong legs and joints

COMPETITION FAVORITE

The Trakehner acquired its athletic and agile physique from earlier crossings with Thoroughbreds and Arabs. In the 1936 Berlin Olympics, the German team won every medal while riding Trakehners. Today, these horses have made a name for themselves in cross-country, jumping, and dressage events.

DRESSAGE COMPETITION

16

ELK-HORN BRAND

ELK-HORN BRAND
The Trakehner was once called the East Prussian because of its origins in what is now a part of Poland. The horses are distinguishable by the elk-horn brand on the nearside quarter.

TEUTONIC KNIGHTS
This ancient order of knights set up the site of the stud at Trakehnan in the 1200s to supply horses for the Crusades.

Powerful quarters help jumping

THE IDEAL HORSE
Today, many consider the Trakehner as being near to the ideal riding or competition horse, with good conformation and a temperament to match. It is highly courageous, and careful breeding has ensured that it has great stamina and endurance.

TRAKEHNER FACTS
• The breed's name comes from the site of the stud at Trakehnan, East Prussia.
• In 1945, over 1,000 Trakehners were led 900 miles (1,450 km) to western Germany to stop them being from captured by the advancing Russians.

LIPIZZANER

THESE BEAUTIFUL horses are usually associated with the famous Spanish Riding School in Vienna – so called because it has always used Spanish horses. The Lipizzaner has been developed as a classical riding horse from five stallions brought from Spain during the 16th century by Archduke Charles II, ruler of the Austro-Hungarian Empire.

Broad, powerful quarters are a feature of the breed

Compact and muscular body with a deep chest

Firm joints and hard grooves

LIPIZZANER AND RIDER
At the Spanish Riding School in Vienna, Lipizzaners are trained over a period of 4–6 years to perform the classical movements of the High School. Lipizzaners may also be used in harness but it is unusual to see them ridden sidesaddle.

AUSTRIAN STUD

The Lipizzaners at the Spanish Riding School are bred at Piber, near Graz, Austria. Eight to ten horses are selected each year.

LIPIZZANER FACTS

• There are about 3,500 Lipizzaner horses in the world.

• The breed is named after the original stud at Lipizza in Slovenia, then part of Austria.

• The horses are a select breed and all are descended from one of five stallions.

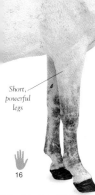

Shoulders are well suited to harness riding

Ramlike profile of the Andalusian is still evident

COLOR CHANGES

Adult Lipizzaners bred at Piber should be all white, but foals are dark brown or black at birth. The horses grow lighter as they mature between the ages of seven and ten. Color variations at other studs are quite common.

Short, powerful legs

White mare and dark brown foal

16

AUSTRALIAN STOCK HORSE

TOUGH AND VERSATILE, the Stock Horse was bred to work under the harsh conditions of the Australian outback. Similar horses have been kept on cattle stations there for nearly 200 years, yet even today the Australian Stock Horse is not considered a standardized breed.

Head is heavy and chunky compared to a Thoroughbred's

Most Stock Horses are bay, but other colours are seen occasionally

STOCK HORSE FACTS

• *Regal Realm*, a famous World Event champion, had a Stock Horse background.

• Stock Horses make up the largest single group of horses in Australia.

• Over 12,000 Walers, sent to fight in World War I, were destroyed after the war ended. Australia's strict quarantine laws prevented their return.

Sloping shoulders are a sign of a good riding horse

Good, sloped pasterns

RECENT BREED
After World War I, there were few horses left in Australia to work on the farms. Some of these horses were crossed with Thoroughbreds and Arabs, giving rise to the Stock Horse. It is still not accepted as a standard breed because of this mixture.

AUSTRALIA

New South Wales

SOUTH PACIFIC OCEAN

COUNTRY OF ORIGIN
Ancestors of the
Australian Stock Horse
were nicknamed Walers
after the southeastern
state of New South Wales
where they worked.

Powerful hindquarters

Well-proportioned legs

16

CHARGE OF THE AUSTRALIAN LIGHT HORSES
During World War I, the British General, Allenby,
used Walers in his campaign against the Turks in
Palestine with great success. A troop of these horses
covered 170 miles (274 km) in four days, while
temperatures reached 100°F (37.8°C).

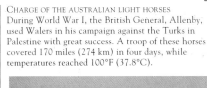

This Australian Stock Horse shows Arab influence

OUTBACK WORK
Rounding up stray
cattle and sheep on
the vast stations of
Australia calls for a
breed with stamina
and endurance. The
first horses brought to
Australia came from
South Africa and then
from Europe. These
were superb riding
horses that could stand
up to the heat.

MORGAN AND DUTCH WARMBLOOD

THESE TWO BREEDS were developed as versatile all-rounders. The Morgan ancestry dates from the late 18th century, whilst the Dutch Warmblood has evolved during the present century as a competition horse.

MORGAN STATUE
The Morgan is much revered in the US. This statue is in the Kentucky Horse Park.

Fine muzzle, with small, firm lips and large nostrils

15

Colors are either bay, brown, black, or chestnut

Ample bone beneath the knee

Wide, deep chest

Long, flowing tail should reach the ground

FIRST MORGAN
The founding stallion of the breed, *Figure*, was born in about 1790 at West Springfield, Massachusetts. In local contests, whether pulling logs or racing, the horse would beat all challengers.

DRESSAGE RIDER
ON DUTCH
WARMBLOOD

COMPETITION HORSES

The Dutch Warmblood was developed from coach horse breeds, but the subsequent Thoroughbred crosses have resulted in competition horses excelling at dressage and jumping.

16

Common colors are brown and bay

Deep body and long back

Good, sound hooves

Well-rounded hooves

Head shape is similar to a Thoroughbred's

DUTCH WARMBLOOD

This horse is a mix of the Dutch Groningen and Gelderlander. The Warmblood was bred specifically to take part in competitions. Famous horses include *Dutch Courage* and Milton.

HEAVY HORSES

INTRODUCTION TO HEAVY HORSES

THE SHEER SIZE and power of the heavy horses makes them instantly recognizable. They include the largest and tallest horses ever bred. Heavy horses have a wide body and a broad back. The shoulders are upright, allowing them to be fitted with a collar, while the chest is broad and powerful.

THE WORKING HORSES
Before mechanization became widespread, heavy horses were very much part of everyday life. Draft, or pulling, horses were harnessed to all kinds of vehicles, from wagons like the one shown here to the first buses and trams. Horses also provided muscle power in factories.

Most heavy horses have feathering on their feet

ITALIAN HEAVY HORSE

Most heavy horses were developed to be strong and to move at a steady pace. The Italian Heavy Horse was mixed with French and English breeds, and is used for light draft work in northern and central Italy.

Body of draft horse is compact and muscular

FORESTRY WORK

Heavy horses are still used in forests around the world for hauling timber. Forestry work is performed better by heavy horses than vehicles, as horses cause less damage to the ground and do not need wide tracks to get into the forest.

PLOW HORSES

Horses have been used for plowing the land since about AD 500, when the Chinese invented a special padded collar for this purpose. This made the heavy horse important to countries that relied on farming for much of their economy.

JUTLAND

CARRYING HEAVILY ARMORED knights into battle was all part of a day's work for the Jutland in medieval times. On more peaceful occasions, this Danish breed was employed on farms, plowing fields and hauling heavy loads over rough tracks. However, increased mechanization means that today Jutlands are rarely seen working the land.

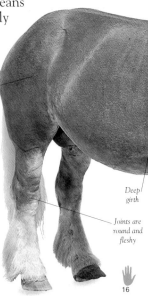

Solid, heavy hindquarters

Deep girth

Joints are round and fleshy

16

STILL IN HARNESS
The Jutland is ideally suited to pulling heavy loads. Although no longer common on farms, some are still used to pull brewers' dray carts through the streets of Denmark.

COAT OF DARK COLORS
The Jutland's dark chestnut coat and
flaxen mane and tail are the result
of crossings with the Suffolk
Punch that first took
place over 100
years ago.

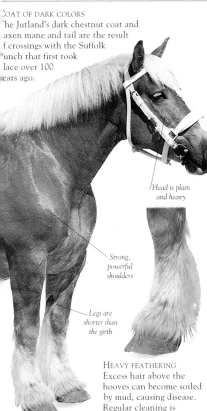

NORTH
SEA
Jutland
Peninsula

DENMARK

COUNTRY OF ORIGIN
These heavy horses
are named after
Denmark's Jutland
Peninsula, where
they were first bred
over 1,000 years ago.
They have been
carefully developed
there ever since.

*Head is plain
and heavy*

*Strong,
powerful
shoulders*

*Legs are
shorter than
the girth*

HEAVY FEATHERING
Excess hair above the
hooves can become soiled
by mud, causing disease.
Regular cleaning is
needed to prevent this.

JUTLAND FACTS

• Viking invaders
brought the forerunners
of the Jutland to
Britain during the 900s.

• Modern Jutlands can
be traced to a British
Suffolk Punch taken to
Denmark in 1860.

• A few Jutlands have
coats colored black,
bay, or roan.

• Though undesirable,
the heavy feathering on
the leg is an easy way to
tell the Jutland from
the Suffolk Punch.

BRABANT

THE HEAVIEST OF the heavy horses, the Brabant is also known as the Belgian Draft. This gentle giant was bred in Europe, but has gained huge popularity in the US since it was first exported there in the 19th century. Brabants have also played a major part in the development of other heavy breeds, such as the English Suffolk Punch.

DIFFERENT TYPES
By the 1870s, there were three groups of Brabants: the *Colosses de la Mahaique* is the most powerful, the *Gris du Hainaut* has a distinctive red roan coloring, and the *Gros de la Dendre* is smaller and lighter than the others.

BRABANT FACTS
• The world's heaviest a Brabant was the American stallion, *Brooklyn Supreme*, who, in 1937, weighed in at 3,200 lb (1,451 kg).
• The Brabant is also called the *race de trait Belge* by the Belgians.
• A heavily pregnant Brabant mare was measured as having a 12 ft (3.65 m) girth.

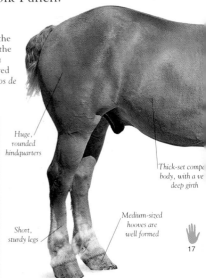

Huge, rounded hindquarters

Thick-set compa body, with a ve deep girth

Medium-sized hooves are well formed

Short, sturdy legs

17

STRONG AND STURDY

An exceedingly strong horse, the Brabant has a tremendously robust, yet short, back and loins. It has huge muscles, important for a draft horse since it spends most of its working life in harness. These characteristics have been carefully maintained by selective breeding.

COUNTRY OF ORIGIN
The Brabant was named after the plains area of Flanders in Belgium where it was developed. Many are now bred in America.

Long, thick mane

Broad chest and short neck

Head is small compared to other heavy horses

Some feathering on lower leg

WORKING THE LAND
The Brabant was once the most famous heavy horse in Europe. During medieval times, it became known as the Flanders Horse and was much in demand as a plow horse. Suited to the variable Belgian climate and working the rich, heavy soil, this colossus was also used to pull farm wagons or dray carts in towns.

PERCHERON

THE FRENCH PECHERON is one of the largest and most elegant of the heavy horses. Once used in battle, on farms, and as a coach horse, it is ridden for pleasure in spite of its huge size. Its strength and willing nature has led to many being exported to work all over the world.

Arched neck is covered by a thick mane

Fine head shape with square, straight profile

Flat nose with broad, open nostrils

Shoulders are unusually long for a heavy horse

Broad, very deep-chested body

Medium sized hoof of hard blue horn

PERCHERON FACTS
• The world's biggest horse was an American Percheron, *Dr Le Gear*, who was 21 hh and weighed 3,024 lb (1,372 kg) in 1908.
• A lighter version of the Percheron was used to haul horse-drawn buses in in Paris the late 19th century.
• Percherons can pull loads of more than 2,205 lb (1,000 kg).

STRENGTH AND BEAUTY
The Percheron's refined shape comes from its crossings with Barb and Arab horses, brought to Europe from North Africa by Moorish invaders in AD 300. Later, Belgian horses helped to give the breed its strength.

Coat is usually chestnut, bay, or brown-bay

NORMAN COB
This breed is a lightweight draft horse. As its name suggests, it was bred in Normandy like the Percheron. At one time, the Cob was a cavalry horse.

COUNTRY OF ORIGIN
The Percheron is named after the area of La Perche in Normandy, one of the great horse-breeding centers of France.

Normandy

FRANCE

ATLANTIC
OCEAN

The tail is docked to prevent reins from catching underneath

17

Lack of feathering on the hooves is unusual for a draft horse

Short, square, powerful body

BRETON
Since medieval times, the Breton has been bred in northwestern France, and its influences include both the Percheron and Ardennais. The Breton is used on farms, especially in the vineyards of the Midi region of France. There were once several types of Bretons, but only two survive today.

CLYDESDALE

POWERFUL HORSES did most of the plowing and heavy work on farms before the days of the steam engine. The Clydesdale was specially bred for this purpose and was exported from Britain to countries all around the world. It is regarded as one of the strongest of the heavy horses.

Long, muscular hindquarters

Head profile is straight and elegant

GOOD MOVER
At one time, the Clydesdale was seen as a type of Shire Horse. Although not as big, the Clydesdale shares the Shire's lively, stylish way of moving.

Hooves covered by heavy, silky feathering

17

BREED FOUNDER

The Clydesdale was developed in the 18th century by the sixth Duke of Hamilton and another breeder, John Paterson. Together, they imported Flemish horses to increase the size and power of the local draught breeds. Later, Shire mares were also involved.

SIXTH DUKE OF HAMILTON

COUNTRY OF ORIGIN

The natural home of the Clydesdale is the Clyde Valley in Lanarkshire, Scotland. Although no longer at work on farms there, some Clydesdales still work in forests in Canada and the Russian Federation.

The rider's uniform is embroidered with gold thread

Silver drums weigh 150 lb (68 kg) each

The rider steers by reins connected to boots and waist

SOUNDS OF WAR

This drum horse is a 15-year-old blue roan Clydesdale. The beating of drums once inspired soldiers as they went into battle, but today the role of the drum horse is ceremonial. These two silver drums were presented to the Household Cavalry of Great Britain by King William IV in 1830.

CLYDESDALE FACTS

• The heaviest and tallest Clydesdale ever recorded weighed 2,800 lb (1,270 kg) and was 20 hh.

• In Michigan, one horse pulled a load of nearly 50 tons (tonnes) over a distance of 1,320 ft (402 m).

• In the days before mechanization, wheat farmers in Canada used teams of about seven horses to pull three-furrowed plows.

SUFFOLK PUNCH

THE TERM "PUNCH" is an old English name for a horse with a barrel-shaped body and short legs. The Suffolk Punch is the oldest of Britain's heavy horses. It was developed in the eastern county of Suffolk during the 1700s. Today, every one of these horses can trace its ancestry back to the first Suffolk, foaled in 1768. The color of the breed is traditionally described "chesnut," without the use of the first "*t*."

Suffolks are bred in seven shades; this example is red.

Lack of feathering keeps mud from clinging to lower leg

WORKING HORSES
The Suffolk Punch was developed as a farm horse, well suited to working the heavy clay soils of eastern England. In spite of its bulk, it can walk a furrow just 9 in (23 cm) wide. The horses are economical to keep and have long, productive lives, with some continuing to work into their twenties.

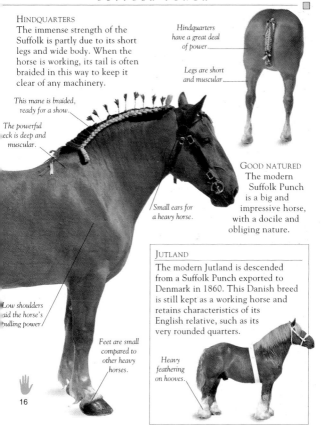

HINDQUARTERS
The immense strength of the Suffolk is partly due to its short legs and wide body. When the horse is working, its tail is often braided in this way to keep it clear of any machinery.

Hindquarters have a great deal of power.

Legs are short and muscular.

This mane is braided, ready for a show.

The powerful neck is deep and muscular.

Small ears for a heavy horse.

GOOD NATURED
The modern Suffolk Punch is a big and impressive horse, with a docile and obliging nature.

Low shoulders aid the horse's pulling power.

Feet are small compared to other heavy horses.

JUTLAND
The modern Jutland is descended from a Suffolk Punch exported to Denmark in 1860. This Danish breed is still kept as a working horse and retains characteristics of its English relative, such as its very rounded quarters.

Heavy feathering on hooves.

16

SHIRE

THE LARGEST OF ALL modern horse breeds, the Shire, is descended from the English Great Horses that were used in medieval times to carry heavily armored knights into battle. The name "Shire" comes from the Midland shire counties of England, from where its ancestors originated.

HEAD DETAIL
The shoulders of the Shire are wide and deep. The neck is quite long for a draft horse, and slightly arched. A broad forehead separates the large, docile eyes that give the Shire its "gentle giant" look.

Back is short and strong

Nose is slightly curved

Deep, wide, shoulders help carry a heavy harness collar

Broad feet covered with a heavy feathering of straight hair

This Beagle gives an idea of the Shire's size

SHIRE FACTS
• In the 1500s, the Shire was influenced by Flanders horses brought to drain the swampy English fenland.
• In 1924, a pair showed a pulling power of 50 tonnes (tons).
• Young Shires are able to work by the time they are three.

17

CART HORSES

Until the mid-1880s, the Shire was known as the English Cart Horse. Its power made it much in demand for pulling carts and working the land. Most Shires can pull loads of up to five tons (tonnes) without difficulty. Today, they can still be seen in English cities, working as draft horses for breweries. In the country, Shires appear at agricultural shows in plowing competitions.

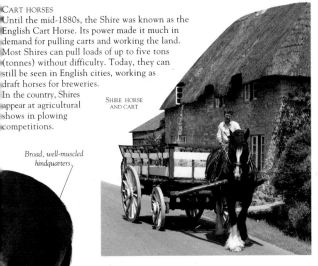

SHIRE HORSE
AND CART

Broad, well-muscled hindquarters

QUICK DEVELOPERS

A Shire has to be at least 16.2 hands high to be registered. It takes around six years for a Shire to grow to its maximum size, with stallions tending to be taller than mares. One Shire, foaled in 1846, grew to more than 21.2 hh by the time it was four and weighed almost 3,360 lb (1,524 kg).

SHIRE
MARE

SHIRE
FOAL

ARDENNAIS

THIS BREED IS regarded as the founder of the European draft horses. It is also called the Ardennes, after the area between France and Belgium where its ancestors lived over 2,000 years ago. One of the oldest heavy breeds, the Ardennais has put its tremendous strength to use on both the farm and the battlefield.

Thick hair on mane

Squared-off, snub nose

Heavy, muscular neck is set back into the shoulders

ARDENNAIS FACTS

• Julius Caesar wrote about this horse in his accounts of the Roman conquest of northern France in 51 BC.

• An artillery horse, it is a veteran of both the French Revolution and World War I.

• The two main types are the heavyweight Ardennais du Nord and the powerful Auxois.

BODY CHARACTERISTICS
The Ardennais has a low, flat forehead that gives it a straight profile. The ears are pricked in an alert manner and the eye sockets are prominent. The wide frame and short legs give an impression of compact strength and power.

Dense feathering above small but powerful feet

ARDENNAIS
ON SHOW

WILLING WORKERS
The Ardennais are gentle horses and are managed easily. They are still hard at work on farms in the Ardennes, where the harsh winters have made them tough. Their ancestors were used by Napoleon's army to carry supplies.

Compact and stocky body shape, with a short back and quarters

Limbs like tree trunks – thick, short, and strong

16

BOULONNAIS

Like the Ardennais, the Boulonnais is also descended from the ancient Forest Horse and developed in northwestern France. However, its Arab blood has given the Boulonnais an elegant appearance, described as looking like polished marble. Most are gray, but others are bay or chestnut.

WILD AND FERAL HORSES

INTRODUCTION TO WILD AND FERAL HORSES

FOUR DIFFERENT GROUPS of horses live in the wild: the true wild horses, zebras, asses, and feral (semiwild) horses. All these species are grazing animals that live in herds. Sadly, though domestic horses have thrived, hunting and the destruction of their habitat have made wild horses increasingly scarce.

DÜLMEN PONY
Some ponies, like the European Dülmen, have roamed in a semiwild state for centuries. Members of this breed have lived at Mierfelder Bruch in Westphalia, Germany since 1316. Although Dülmens resemble the British New Forest Pony, there is no link between the two breeds.

ZEBRAS
All three types of zebras live in Africa. They are easily recognized their black and white stripes, whic serve as a form of camouflage.

Kulans can go 2–3 days without water

Kulans can run at speeds up to 40 mph (65 km/h)

KULAN ASSES

Wild asses live in Africa and Asia. They prefer dry, stony habitats, where they feed on grass and shrubs. Kulans are a subspecies of onagers and live in small numbers in Turkmenistan, east of the Caspian Sea.

WILD HORSE FACTS

• Herds of wild asses have been known to number up to 1,000 animals.

• Not all zebras have stripes; some are pure black. Although rare, these live alongside their striped cousins.

• Wild horses usually spend 60–80 percent of their time looking for food.

FERAL HORSES

In some places, domestic horses that escaped into the wild have formed feral herds. These animals are rounded up occasionally to check their health.

PRZEWALSKI'S HORSE

THIS ASIAN WILD horse was discovered in 1881 by a Russian colonel who gave the breed its name. It is an important link between the early types of wild horses and today's modern breeds.

RUSSIAN EXPLORER

Colonel N. M. Przewalsk (1839–88) was a Russia soldier and explorer. By the time he mad his discovery, the horse was already in decline; it wa extinct in the wild by 1969.

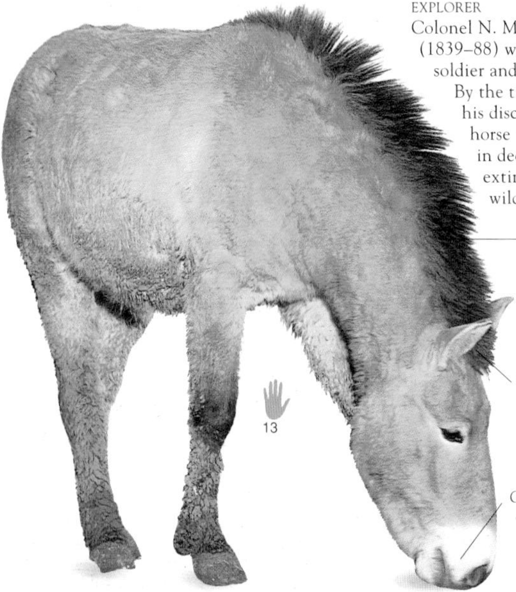

Sparse, shor mane grows upright and is always partly black

Short forelock does not reach eyes

Colored speckle on muzzle and around eyes

13

CAPTIVE SURVIVORS

In 1900, Przewalski's Horses were first kept at the Askania-Nova Zoo, in the Ukraine – where the largest group lives today. In 1959, a breeding programe was started with the goal of reestablishing these horses in the wild. Today, there are more than 1,450 Przewalski's horses worldwide.

AREA OF DISCOVERY

Przewalski discovered this horse in the area of the Tachin Schah (the Mountains of the Yellow Horses") south of the Gobi Desert in Mongolia.

TARPAN

This illustration shows a Tarpan, another Asian wild horse. Although extinct in the wild by 1879, some were kept and crossbred by Polish farmers. Recently, horses with the greatest likeness to their ancestors have helped recreate semiwild herds.

ZEBRA

THE STRIPED PATTERN of the zebra makes it instantly recognizable. All three types of zebras live in Africa, but in different areas. Grevy's Zebras can be found in the far north, the Plains Zebras roam the grasslands to the east, and the Mountain Zebras inhabit the uplands of the south.

GREVY'S ZEBRA
This is the largest zebra, standing 5 ft (1.6 m) tall at the shoulder. It is an endangered species – only about 5,000 remain

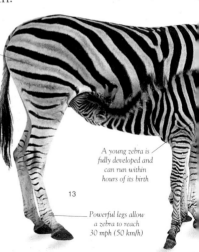

Striped coat helps individual zebras blend together in a herd

ZEBRA FACTS
• Zebras have good hearing, but they also rely on nearby animals – ostriches for sight and wildebeest for smell – to help warn them of approaching danger.

• Zebras lash out with their feet to defend themselves against predators such as lions.

• Mountain zebras may soon become extinct. There are only about 2,000 left in the wild.

A young zebra is fully developed and can run within hours of its birth

13

Powerful legs allow a zebra to reach 30 mph (50 km/h)

PLAINS ZEBRA
These are the most common zebras, and herds can still be seen in most African wildlife reserves. Zebras look after each other and if one member of the group is missing, the others will search for it.

Mane stands up on back of neck

TAME ZEBRAS
A few zebras have been trained to pull carriages. This 19th century scene shows a team of four zebras pulling a trader's vehicle, but these examples were usually gimmicks performed by publicity-conscious companies. In rare cases, zebras have been broken and ridden.

Mare and foal stay together for about five months

QUAGGA
A close relative of the plains zebra, the quagga lived in southern Africa. It was hunted to extinction, with the last survivor dying in 1883. Attempts are now being made to re-breed a quaggalike animal from plains zebras.

ASS, DONKEY, MULE, AND HINNY

PAIRINGS OF HORSES and wild asses have been carried out for centuries to produce working animals that are strong, yet more sure-footed than the horse. The donkey is the domesticated form of the African wild ass. A mule has a donkey father and a horse mother. A hinny has a horse father and donkey mother.

Shaggy coat

Light-colored underside

Short brown mane

Light-colored legs blend into the background.

WORKING DONKEYS
Donkeys are very strong and have been used for pulling carts in Ireland for centuries. To help them cope with the colder northern climate, these donkeys have grown thick coats.

AFRICAN WILD ASS
The ass is the ancestor of the donkey. These asses live in herds in hot, dry regions of northern Africa.

EUROPEAN DONKEY AND CART

DOMESTIC DONKEYS
Many donkeys are kept
as pets. They are social
animals and should not
be kept alone.

Large ears

Muscular neck
and heavy head

Strong,
sturdy legs

Mule's stubbornness
stems from its
wariness of people.

Hooves
can become
overgrown if the
donkey lives at
pasture.

MULE
Mules were first
bred in the Middle
East about 4,000
years ago. They have strong herd instincts and so
work better in packs than by themselves. These
groups are called mule trains.

Mane is closer in
shape to a donkey's
than a horse's

HINNY
Hinnies live for
up to 40 years.
Although they are
usually sterile, on
occasion they have
been known to
produce foals.

Color
can vary

DONKEY FACTS
• Donkeys bred in the
Poitou region of France
and Spain are among
the largest in the world
at 56 in (142 cm).

• The largest donkey
ever recorded lived in
Glasgow, Scotland, in
1902, and was 84 in
(213 cm) high.

• Miniature donkeys
less than 34 in (86 cm)
tall live on the
Mediterranean islands
of Sardinia and Sicily.

FERAL HORSES

DOMESTIC ANIMALS that have
returned to the wild are described
as feral. Many horses around the
world have either escaped from
their owners or have been
abandoned. If they remain
uncontrolled, feral horses can cause
great damage through overgrazing
and trampling on crops.

CHRISTOPHER COLUMBUS
The early American feral
horses were descendants
of Spanish horses taken
to the New World by
Columbus in 1493.

CAMARGUES
These white horses live in the coastal marshes of the
Rhône delta, southern France, where they survive on
a meager, salty diet. They are ridden by French
gardians (cowboys).

FERAL FACTS

• There were an
estimated five million
feral horses in the
US in the late
16th century.

• Small, dun-colored
feral horses living in
Colombia are possibly
descendants of horses
brought by the Spanish
conquistadors.

• Camargues are
sometimes called
"the horses of the sea."

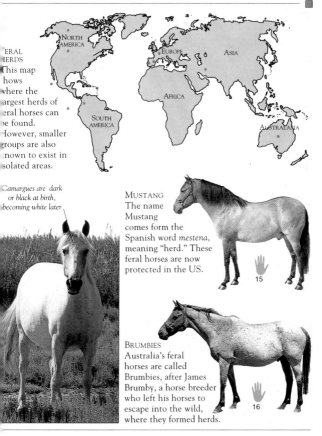

Camargues are dark
or black at birth,
becoming white later

MUSTANG
The name
Mustang
comes form the
Spanish word *mestena*,
meaning "herd." These
feral horses are now
protected in the US.

15

BRUMBIES
Australia's feral
horses are called
Brumbies, after James
Brumby, a horse breeder
who left his horses to
escape into the wild,
where they formed herds.

16

133

REFERENCE
SECTION

HORSE CLASSIFICATION

WITHIN THE GROUP of animals known as mammals, horses form part of a smaller group, the Perissodactyla, or odd-toed mammals. Members of this group include rhinoceroses, with three toes on each limb, as well as single-hooved horses. Within this category, zebras, asses, and horses make up a small family called Equidae. Each species can breed with other members of the family and their offspring are called hybrids.

PART OF THE FAMILY
Although part of the horse family Equidae, the mule is classified as a hybrid. In most cases, hybrids are sterile. Ponies are grouped with domestic horses, as they can breed with horses and produce fertile offspring.

MULE

HYBRIDS
These are offspring that have parents from two different species. Some crosses are deliberate and aim to combine qualities of both parents. Zebroids, for example, may be more suitable for working in the dry, hot African climate than horses.

MALE DONKEY	+	FEMALE HORSE	=	MULE
MALE HORSE	+	FEMALE DONKEY	=	HINNY
ZEBRA	+	HORSE	=	ZEBROID
ZEBRA	+	DONKEY	=	ZEDONK

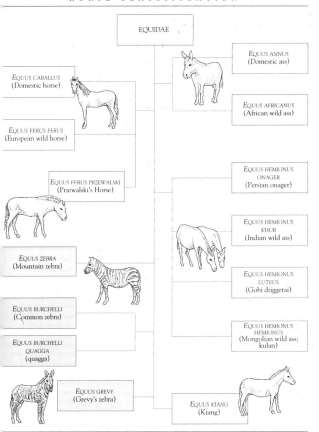

EQUIDAE

EQUUS ASINUS
(Domestic ass)

EQUUS AFRICANUS
(African wild ass)

EQUUS CABALLUS
(Domestic horse)

EQUUS FERUS FERUS
(European wild horse)

EQUUS FERUS PRZEWALSKI
(Przewalski's Horse)

*EQUUS HEMIONUS
ONAGER*
(Persian onager)

*EQUUS HEMIONUS
KHUR*
(Indian wild ass)

*EQUUS HEMIONUS
LUTEUS*
(Gobi dziggetai)

EQUUS ZEBRA
(Mountain zebra)

EQUUS BURCHELLI
(Common zebra)

*EQUUS BURCHELLI
QUAGGA*
(quagga)

*EQUUS HEMIONUS
HEMIONUS*
(Mongolian wild ass;
kulan)

EQUUS GREVY
(Grevy's zebra)

EQUUS KIANG
(Kiang)

RECORDS AND FACTS

THE SHEER DIVERSITY of horse types and breeds spread around the world has led to a number of quite amazing facts and figures. Although some are natural phenomena, many are connected with the horse's association with people, a relationship that goes back over 6,000 years.

• The tallest known horse was an English Shire called *Mammoth*, which stood at 21.2 hands high.

• The US Pony Express ran from Missouri to California, a distance of 1,966 miles (3,164 km). This was covered by 400 ponies in a relay over 10 days.

• When spoken to, horses distinguish tones rather than particular words.

• Shetland pit ponies worked underground for around 20 years.

• The oldest known Thoroughbred was a chestnut gelding called *Tango Duke*. It was born in 1935 in Victoria, Australia and lived for 42 years.

• The game of polo originated in Persia over 2,500 years ago and was played by both men and women.

• The smallest and lightest horse in the world was reckoned to be *Little Pumpkin*, a miniature horse foaled in the US in 1973. When two years old, it was 3.5 hands high and weighed just over 20 lb (9 kg).

• The heaviest weight ever pulled by two horses was recorded in 1893, when two Clydesdales pulled a load weighing 131 tons (131 tonnes). But recent estimates put the load at about 50 tons (45 tonnes).

• The most recently discovered breed was the Caspian pony, found in Iran in 1965.

• In 1277, a *destrier*, or trained battle charger, cost roughly the equivalent of a modern limousine. Less powerful horses were only a third as much.

• Horses can breed throughout their lives. The oldest horse ever to give birth was a 42 year-old Australian brood mare.

• The longest mane belonged to a horse from California, called *Maud*. It grew to a length of 18 ft (5.5 m).

• Today there are over 150 different horse and pony breeds, as well as many crossbred types.

• The longest tail, measuring 22 ft (6.7 m), was grown by an American Palomino called *Chinook*.

• The top-earning movie horse was *Tony* "the Wonder Horse." With cowboy film star Tom Mix (1880–1940), Tony earned around $8 million in almost 300 films until injury ended his career in 1932.

• Zebras have stripes that evolved originally as camouflage to break up the body outline.

• Horses were first used for public transportation in Britain in 1564.

• The first recorded race with mounted horses was at the Greek Olympiad in 624 BC.

• Horses were first shod in Roman times by Celtic mercenaries.

• In England, people drive cars on the left. This custom stems from coaching days, when drivers drove on the left to prevent their whip (which was held in the right hand) becoming entangled in hedgerows bordering the side of the road.

• Horses have two blind spots. One is directly behind them and the other is right in front of the end of their nose.

• The last horse-drawn passenger train ran over the Fintona branch line in Northern Ireland, which closed in 1957.

• Rodeos began in the 19th century as informal contests between American cowboys. The first attempt to stage a world cup rodeo contest was in 1982, in Australia.

• Genghis Khan operated the Yam – mounted messengers who crossed the Mongol Empire, covering 150 miles (242 km) a day.

• Millions of acres of American farmland were harvested with huge machines drawn by teams of up to 24 horses.

• In 1286 BC at the battle of Kadesh, in present-day Syria, the Hittites used 3,500 horsedrawn chariots in their defeat of Rameses I of Egypt.

LEARNING TO RIDE

RIDING CAN BE ENJOYED at any level, from a gentle hack in the country to taking part in national competitions. The rider progresses through different stages and learns how to control the horse while developing balance and rhythm. Having a good instructor and learning the correct methods from the start is the best way to begin.

RIDING SCHOOL
The ideal place to learn to ride is at a registered riding school with qualified instructors who can help riders correct their mistakes quickly.

EQUIPMENT
Riders should dress for safety and comfort. Some special items may be needed for riding in the dark.
1 Warm jumper for cold weather. 2 Tweed hacking jacket for everyday wear. 3 Hard hat covered with silk.
4 Stretch jodhpurs for freedom of movement.
5 Jodhpur boots.
6 Long leather, or rubber boots. 7 Gloves.
8 Stirrup light.
9 Fluorescent belt for night riding. 10 Cross-country whip.

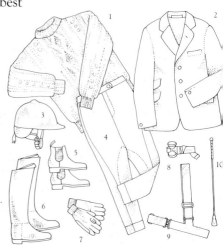

MOUNTING UP

1 Stand on left of horses facing tail. Hold reins in left hand placed in front of saddle and turn stirrup iron outward.

2 Put left foot into stirrup iron and face horse's side. Hold bottom of mane with right hand and push off ground with right leg.

3 Swing right leg over horse's back, turn body to face forward and lower body into saddle. Place right foot in stirrup iron.

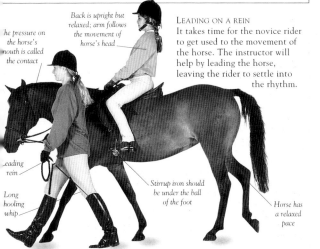

LEADING ON A REIN
It takes time for the novice rider to get used to the movement of the horse. The instructor will help by leading the horse, leaving the rider to settle into the rhythm.

Back is upright but relaxed; arm follows the movement of horse's head

he pressure on the horse's mouth is called the contact

eading rein

Long hooling whip

Stirrup iron should be under the ball of the foot

Horse has a relaxed pace

The different gaits

A horse moves its legs in a different sequence for each change of pace, from a trot to a canter to a gallop. Riders must learn to keep their body movements in time with the rhythm of the horse.

TROT

CANTER

Sit deeply in the saddle

Keep the rein in contact with horse's mouth

GALLOP

Stirrups must be shortened

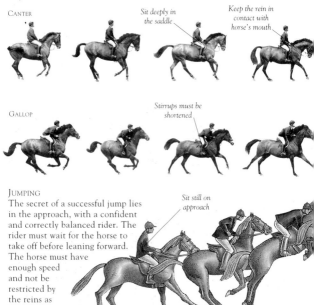

JUMPING

The secret of a successful jump lies in the approach, with a confident and correctly balanced rider. The rider must wait for the horse to take off before leaning forward. The horse must have enough speed and not be restricted by the reins as it jumps.

Sit still on approach

Keep hands still

TROT

The trot is quite a bumpy movement. Riders learn to let the horse throw them up in the saddle and land back lightly.

Press with the inside of the legs to help keep horse moving

CANTER

The rider's back is relaxed to move in harmony with the rocking motion of the horse. The hands follow the movement of the horse's head.

Lean forward from the hips

Hands stay on either side of neck

GALLOP

The rider sits forward and rises slightly out of the saddle to take the weight off the horse's back, allowing it to go faster.

Keep head up and eyes straight ahead

Make sure lower legs are held straight under the body

CHOOSING A HORSE

OWNING A HORSE requires considerable commitment, both in time and money. The horse must above all be suitable for the purpose in mind. It is better to buy privately rather than at an auction since this allows a closer inspection. The horse should be ridden and then checked closely by a vet before a final decision is made.

FURTHER EXPENSES

Apart from the cost of the horse, there will be stabling, food, and veterinary bills. You will also need to buy equipment, such as tack and clothing.

9–10 YEARS   15 YEARS

19–20 YEARS   20–25 YEARS

TEETH

The front teeth can be used to tell the age of a horse. As the horse ages, the slope of the teeth increases and they become discolored.

Saddle must fit properly

Horses need to be shod every four to six weeks

Riding clothing can be expensive

WHAT TO LOOK FOR

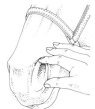

NOSE
The nostrils should have large air passages and be thin and flexible. When the horse is at rest, they should be almost closed. If not, there could be a breathing problem.

EYES
Poor eyesight can cause a horse to shy away from things. The eyes should be clear and free from tears, the pupils black, and the eyelids thin and smooth.

TEETH
The front teeth should be level; otherwise, the horse will be unable to graze properly. Check for damage in the mouth caused by an unsuitable bit or sharp teeth.

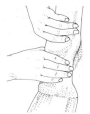

HOOFS
The wall of the hoof should be smooth, not cracked or brittle. The hoof must be symmetrical, with the shoes worn evenly – an uneven fit might indicate a defect.

LEGS
The tendons should be hard and sinewy and not soft and puffy. Soreness or swelling is a sign of a recent or previous injury. Trotting on a leading rein may show lameness.

COAT
Check for swellings and blemishes on the back, often made by a badly fitting saddle. The coat should be clean and shiny. A dull, scaly coat is the result of parasites.

HORSE CARE

A STABLED HORSE needs
constant grooming. This not
only improves its looks, but
also keeps the horse healthy
and feeling good. Horses
living in fields develop oils,
giving their coat a natural
gloss that can be removed by
continual washing.

STABLE RUBBER

DANDY BRUSH

BODY BRUSH

WATER BRUSH

SWEAT SCRAPER

HOOF OIL AND BRUSH

HOOF PICK

METAL CURRY COMB

PLASTIC CURRY COMB

MANE COMB

SPONGE

WASH AND BRUSH UP

Stabled horses should be groomed thoroughly
at least once a day. Grooming includes a
number of tasks and special tools are needed
to do each job properly.

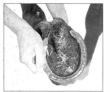

CLEANING HOOVES

Clean the horse's hooves
out every day using a hoof
pick. This removes any
matter that could
collect moisture and allow
germs to infect the hoof.

SPONGING THE FACE

Using water and a
special sponge, clean
the nose, eyes, and lips
separately. Wash the
sponge out thoroughly
afterward.

COMBING THE TAIL

After untangling any
knots, brush out the tail
carefully so as not to pull
out any hairs. A damp
brush will flatten the short
hairs at the top.

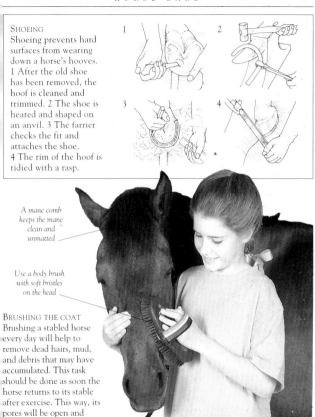

SHOEING

Shoeing prevents hard surfaces from wearing down a horse's hooves. 1 After the old shoe has been removed, the hoof is cleaned and trimmed. 2 The shoe is heated and shaped on an anvil. 3 The farrier checks the fit and attaches the shoe. 4 The rim of the hoof is tidied with a rasp.

A mane comb keeps the mane clean and unmatted

Use a body brush with soft bristles on the head

BRUSHING THE COAT

Brushing a stabled horse every day will help to remove dead hairs, mud, and debris that may have accumulated. This task should be done as soon the horse returns to its stable after exercise. This way, its pores will be open and easier to clean.

Finishing touches

Extra attention can be given to a horse if it is to be prepared for a show. After washing, the mane and tail can be braided. This also helps the mane fall in the right way later. Oiling the hooves makes them look smart. Bandages are used to protect the horse's legs when it is being transported and give it extra support and warmth during exercise. The coat can be made to look more attractive by careful clipping and combing.

1 BRAIDING A MANE
Dampen the mane and braid it in sections, starting at the top.

2 ROLLING UP
Pass a needle through the bottom of each braid and roll it up.

3 FINISHING OFF
Push needle through knot and wind thread round to hold it in place.

BRAIDING A TAIL
Start the braid at the top and gradually work down, with the ends forming a long pigtail. Secure this with an elastic band and turn it up into a loop, which is then stitched to form a double braid. Make sure it is not too tight.

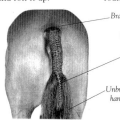

Braid whole tail to the bottom of the dock.

Continue braid to the end of the tail and sew back in a double braid

Unbraided hair hangs loose.

CLIPPING AND COMBING

The type of clip a horse receives depends on the sort of work it will do and how much it sweats. For a show, patterns may be made on a horse's rear by combing through a template in a different direction from the rest of the coat.

CHECKERBOARD COMB

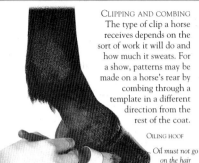

OILING HOOF

Oil must not go on the hair above the hoof.

Hoof brush

CHASER CLIP

HOOF CARE

Applying hoof oil to the hoof's wall prevents it from losing moisture and becoming dry and brittle, as well as smartening its appearance. As the hoof grows, it will need trimming to prevent the wall from becoming too long and splitting.

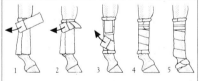

HUNTER CLIP

BANDAGING LEGS

Leg bandages are wrapped over a soft lint padding. 1 Start from the top. 2 Wrap bandage in same direction as padding. 3 Finish off midway up the pastern. 4 Exercise bandage helps support the tendons. 5 Stable bandage prevents damage.

SHARK'S TEETH COMB

DRAWING A HORSE

SKETCHING OR painting a horse is a good way to become familiar with the shape of its body. Practice from pictures before drawing a real horse, which will move about. First, draw a quick outline and fill in the details later. Experiment with different techniques, including charcoal and pencil. When confident, try using some colored inks.

ARTIST'S TOOLS
You will need a set of basic artist's tools. 1 Drawing pencil. 2 Selection of colored pencils. 3 Eraser. 4 Clipboard and paper. 5 Thick pencil. 6 Ink pen. 7 Willow charcoal. 8 Pencil sharpener. 9 Colored inks.

DRAWING THE HEAD
The horse's face not only reveals its breed but can be surprisingly expressive and full of character. Try to capture some of this in your sketch. Much of the head is made up of small circular lines. Rehearse a line before actually drawing it. Carefully mark where short or long lines will finish, and use these marks as guides.

1 Begin by drawing the outline of the nose. These vertical lines provide a good reference point for the other features.

2 As you build up the structure of the head, draw small, faint, circular lines to give overall shape to the cheeks and eye sockets.

THE WHOLE HORSE
Try to capture the whole of
the horse at a glance. Draw it
quickly to suggest fluidity and
agility. At first, sketch very
loosely and lightly, using a
pencil to get the shape of each
part of the body.

1 With eyes half-closed,
sketch an outline of
the body and neck.
Concentrate on the
shape of the muscles,
especially around the
quarters, which will
convey a sense of power.

2 Make sure the horse's
hindquarters are
slightly higher than the
front shoulders. Then
start the legs and head.

3 Look at the shapes
created by the spaces
between the body and
legs, to help you find the
correct proportions.

4 Finally, shade in the
details of the body.
Shadows emphasize the
muscles and give the
horse a solid look.

3 Complete the
outline with rounded
strokes to form the
mane, mouth, cheek,
and ears. Keep the lines
light at this stage.

4 Now draw in the
eyes, fetlock, and
nostrils. These major
features start to suggest
the horse's character
and expression.

5 Using the guide
lines, add shading
to give the head
three-dimensional
form. Erase any
unwanted guidelines.

Resources

American Association of Equine Practitioners
4075 Iron Works Parkway
Lexington, KY 40511
(859) 233-0147

American Endurance Ride Conference
148 Maple Street
Auburn, CA 95603
(530) 823-2260

American Horse Council
1616 H Street NW
Washington, DC 20006
(202) 296-4031

American Horse Protection Association
1000 29th Street NW
#T-100
Washington, DC 20007
(202) 965-0500

USA Equestrian
4047 Iron Works Parkway
Lexington, KY 40511
(859) 258-2472

American Quarter Horse Association
P.O. Box 200
Amarillo, TX 79168
(800) 376-4811

American Riding Instructor Association
28801 Trenton Court
Bonita Springs, FL 34134
(239) 948-3232

American Saddlebred Horse Association
4093 Iron Works Parkway
Lexington, KY 40511
(859) 259-2742

Arabian Horse Registry of America
12000 Zuni Street
Westminster, CO 80234
(303) 450-4748

Harness Tracks of America Inc.
4640 East Sunrise
Ste. 200
Tucson, AZ 85718
(520) 529-2525

The Jockey Club
(Thoroughbreds)
821 Corporate Drive
Lexington, KY 40503
(859) 224-2700

Jockey's Guild, Inc.
250 West Main Street
Lexington, KY 40507
(859) 259-3211

Kentucky Horse Park
4089 Iron Works Parkway
Lexington, KY 40511
(859) 233-4303

North American Riding for the Handicapped Association
P.O. Box 33150
Denver, CO 80233
(800) 369-RIDE

The Professional
Rodeo Cowboy's
Association
101 Pro Rodeo Drive
Colorado Springs,
CO 80919
(719) 593-8840

Tennessee Walking
Horse Breeders' and
Exhibitors'
Association
P.O. Box 286
Lewisburg, TN 37091
(800) 359-1574

United States
Dressage Federation
220 Lexington Green
Circle
Lexington, KY 40503
(859) 971-2277

United States
Trotting Association
(Standardbreds)
750 Michigan Avenue
Columbus, OH 43215
(614) 224-2291

Thoroughbred
Owners' and
Breeders' Association
P.O. Box 4367
Lexington, KY 40544
(859) 276-2291

United States Polo
Association
771 Corporate Drive
Lexington, KY 40503
(859) 219-1000

Thoroughbred Racing
Association of North
America
420 Fair Hill Drive
Elkton, MD 21921
(410) 392-9200

United States
Eventing Association
525 Old Waterford
Rd. NW
Leesburg, VA 20176
(703) 779-0440

United States
Equestrian Team
Pottersville Road
Gladstone, NJ 07934
(908) 234-1251

CANADA

Breed Associations:

Canadian
Thoroughbred Horse
Society—Ontario
Division
P.O. Box 172
Rexdale ON
M9W 5L1
(416) 675-3602

Canadian Quarter
Horse Association
Box 1122
Carberry MB R0K 0H0
(204) 834-2479

Sport Horses:

Canadian Sport
Horse Association
Box 1625
Holland Landing ON
L9N 1P2
(905) 830-9288

Standardbred Canada
2150 Meadowvale Blvd.
Mississauga ON
L5N 6R6
(905) 858-3060

Glossary

ACTION
The way a horse moves its body.

AGED
A horse of seven or more years old.

AGING
Estimating the age of a horse from its teeth.

AIDS
Signals made by the rider to communicate with the horse.

BLEMISH
Permanent mark caused by injury or disease.

BLINKERS
Flaps on the bridle to ensure the horse can only see straight ahead.

BLOOD STOCK
A racing Thoroughbred.

BLUE FEET
Blue-black coloring of the horn on the hooves of some breeds.

BONE
Circumference around the leg beneath the knee or hock, which influences the ability of the horse to carry weight. Used in the term "big boned."

BREAKING-IN
The initial training of a horse, to allow it to be ridden or harnessed.

BREED
A group bred selectively for particular features over many generations, and recognized on the basis of these characteristics.

BRIDLE
Equipment used to control a horse's head.

BROOD MARE
A mare used for breeding.

BRUSHING
A conformational fault, with the hoof or shoe striking the opposite fetlock.

BUCK
Leaping into the air: the back is kept arched, and the horse lands on its stiff forelegs.

CARRIAGE HORSE
A light horse used for pulling carriages.

CHESTNUT
The horny, oval-shaped area on the inside of the forelegs and hocks.

COLD-BLOODED
Horses with ancestors originating from the cold climates of northwestern Europe.

COLLAR
Part of a harness worn by a heavy horse for pulling loads.

COLT
Ungelded male horse under four years old.

CONFORMATION
The shape and proportions of the horse's body.

CROSSBREEDING
The mating of two horses of different breeds or types.

DAM
Mother horse.

DORSAL STRIPE
Dark hairs extending down the back toward the tail.

EQUIDAE
Family of mammals comprising all horses, ponies, asses, and zebras.

ERGOT
Horny growth located on the back of the fetlock.

FARRIER
Someone who makes horseshoes and who shoes horses.

FETLOCK
A tuft of hair that grows above a horse's hoof.

FILLY
A female horse under four years old.

FOAL
A horse under a year old.

FORELEGS
The front two legs of a horse.

FROG
The triangular-shaped pad on the bottom of the horse's foot that acts as a shock absorber.

GAIT
The way a horse moves.

GELDING
Castrated male horse.

GIRTH
Circumference of a horse's body measured from behind the withers.

HOCKS
Bones forming the knees of the rear legs.

HARNESS
Collective term for equipment used to control a draft horse.

HAUNCHES
The hips and buttocks.

HOT-BLOODED
Horses with ancestors originating from hot Middle Eastern countries,

MANE
Long hair on the back of a horse's neck.

MARTINGALE
Item of tack used to increase control of a horse's head, or to alter the pull of the reins.

MARE
A female horse more than four years old.

MULE
Offspring of a male donkey and female horse.

NEARSIDE
The left side of a horse, where it is usual to saddle-up and mount.

OFFSIDE
The right side of a horse.

PEDIGREE
The ancestry of the individual horse.

POINTS
External features, responsible for the horse's conformation.

PONY
A horse not exceeding 14.2 hh.

PUREBRED
A thoroughbred.

REINS
The strap attached to the bit.

SADDLE PAD
Pad placed under the saddle to prevent chafing or rubbing.

STALLION
An ungelded male horse over four years old.

STUD
A stallion kept for breeding.

STUD BOOK
The breed society's record, featuring the pedigrees of purebred stock.

TACK
All saddlery, riding, and driving equipment.

TYPE
A horse that fulfills a specific function, rather than a specific breed, for example, Hunter Type.

WARMBLOOD
Horses that are half- or part-bred, resulting from thoroughbred and Arabian crosses with other breeds.

WITHERS
Part of the horse above the shoulders, where the neck joins with the body.

Index

Acknowledgments

Dorling Kindersley would like to thank:
Hilary Bird for the index;
Kristin Ward, Deslie Lawrence, Marian
Rickerby, Elwyn Hartley Edwards, and
Tim Hetherington for editorial assistance.

Special photography by:
Akhil Bakhshi; Peter Chadwick; Gordon
Clayton; Steve Gorton; Kit Houghton; Colin
Keates, Natural History Museum, London 24-5,
77tc, 127br, 129br; Bob Langrish; Ray Moller;
Tracy Morgan; Stephen Oliver 91-2; Tim
Ridley; Karl Shone; Jerry Young.

Illustrations by:
Joanna Cameron; Tony Graham; Will Giles;
John Hutchinson; Janos Marffy; Sean Milne;
Sandra Pond; John Temerton; John Woodcock;
Debra Woodward.

Picture credits:
t=top b=bottom c=center l=left r=right
Animal Photography/Sally-Anne Thompson
69cr, 89tr, 108cl;/R. Willbie 124bl, 132br.
Bridgeman 86bl. Bruce Coleman/Steve C.
Kaufmann 125tc/Fritz Prenzel 76-77, 82bl;/
Jonathan Wright 122-123. Susan Daniel 73tc.
ET Archive 101cr. Mary Evans 97tr, 126tr, 129tr,
132tr. Werner Forman Archive 71cr. Hamilton
Collection, Lennoxlove House, Haddington,
Scotland 115tl. Robert Harding 13tr, 54bl, 56cl.
Michael Holford 14cr & br, 15cl. Kit Houghton
48-49, 52bl, 60br, 65br, 67tl, 83tc, 94bl, 104-105,
116cl. Bob Langrish 31cl, 35tl, 53br, 59b, 90bl,
93br, 107bl & bc, 119tr, 121tc, 124br. Peter
Newark's American Pictures 89br. Only Horses
36br. Oxford Scientific Films/ M. Austerman
127tl. "Complete Guide to Equitation" by
Norman Thelwell published by Methuen,
London. Zefa 99br.

Horse names and owners:
3br *Rajah*, West Midlands Mounted Police; 10-1
Barone, Mr Tavazzani; 21cl *Duke*, Jim
Lockwood; 22-3 *Brutt*, R. Oliver; 34tr *Lyphento*,
Conkwell Stud; 40-41 *Quist and Rajah*, West
Midlands Police; 41tl *Nibble*, Kinstroop; 50-51
Lockinge Edward, Abigail Hampton; 53tr *Little
Trouble*, M. McCabe; 52-53 *Parlington Pepsi &
Dulcie*, Mrs Johnston; 54-5 *Little Elska*, G & H

Greenfield; 55br *Blue Print*, Mervyn & Pauline
Ramage; 56-7 *Warrendale Duke*, Mr Dickson;
57tr *Waverhead William*, Mr & Mrs Errington;
57br *Sunbeam Superstar*, David Vyse; 59t *Blyth
Jessica*, M. Houlden; 58 *Murrayton Delphimus*,
June Freeman; 61 *Bowerwood Aquila*, Mrs Rae
Turner; 62 *Blackhill Sparkle*, Mrs Crump; 63
Malibu Park Command Performance, K & L
Sinclair; 64-5 *Spinway Bright Morning*, S.
Hodgkins; 65tr *Llanarth Sally*, Mr & Mrs Bigley;
66 *Chi Chi*, Steve White; 67 *Clover*, Kenneth
Burton; 68 *Dimolino*, J. Waldherr; 68-9 *Nomad*,
Miss Helen Blair; Hopstone Shabiz, Mrs Scott;
72-3 *Pegasus, Cleopatra and Bernando of
Kilverstone*, Lady Fisher; 75br *Ausdan Svejk*, J.
Goddard Fenwick and Lyn Moran; 78t *Skippers
Valentine*, T J Crouch; 81br *Montemere-O-Nova*
Nan Thurman; 81tr *Sjouke*, Sonia Gray; 82-3
Ardent Lodger, Mr & Mrs Duffy; 83br *Restif*,
Haras National De Compiègne, France; 85 tr,br
Wychwood Dynascha, Mrs G. Harwood; 84tr,
84-5 *Hit Man*, Boyd Cantrell; 88bl *Doc's
Maharaja*, Harold Bush; 93tr *Campanero XXIV*,
Nigel Oliver; 94-5 *Oaten Mainbrace*, Mr & Mrs
Dimmock; 95tr *Samurai*, H. Eppinger; 96-7
Muschamp Mauersee, J. Lorch; 98-99 *Saglavy
Szella*, J. Goddard Fenwick and Lyn Moran; 100
Scrulo Victory, Mrs Waller; 102b *Shaker's
Supreme*, Fred & Bonnie Neuville; 103br *Tokyo
Joe*, Lorna Tew; 108-9 J. Nielsen; 110-1 Roy
Kentucky Horse Park, USA; 113br *Tango &*
112-3 *Ibis*, Haras National de San Lô, France;
114 *Blue Print*, Mervyn & P. Ramage; 116-7
Laurel Keepsake II, P. Adams & Sons; 117tr
Tempo, J. Neilsen; 118-9 Jim Lockwood; 120-1
Ramses du Vallon Haras, National de Pau,
France; 121br *Urus*, Haras National de
Compiègne; 133cr *Patrick*, Kentucky Horse
Park; 133br *Pone*, Ron & Anna Baker; 146bl
Ovation, Robert Oliver.

Every effort has been made to trace the
copyright holders and we apologize for any
unintentional omissions. We would be pleased
to insert the appropriate acknowledgments in
any subsequent edition of this publication.

All other images © Dorling Kindersley
For further information see:
www.dkimages.com